The Bassist's Guide to Creativity

Expand Your Groove Potential

by Chris Kringel

ISBN 978-1-4234-0556-6

7777 W. Bluemound Rd. P.O. Box 13819 Milwaukee, WI 53213

In Australia Contact:
Hal Leonard Australia Pty. Ltd.
4 Lentara Court
Cheltenham, Victoria, 3192 Australia
Email: ausadmin@halleonard.com.au

Visit Hal Leonard Online at
www.halleonard.com

Contents

Introduction

Welcome to the *Bassist's Guide to Creativity*! This book will help open up your creativity and realize your own potential. I ask and challenge you to read from beginning to end and to complete each exercise. Please do not skim through, thinking you will get the full benefit of this book. Much thought and creativity went into the method, exercises, and order. Although this book is written with the electric bass in mind, if you play upright it will also be of use since the ideas and approaches are about creativity.

In this book we will explore what parts of your creativity are easy for you to access and what areas you might want to work on. A major step to opening up the creative process is becoming aware about who you are, how you think, and what you want. I cannot stress enough the importance of being open to the exercises; give them all a try. What do you have to lose? You could be rid of the things that hold back your creativity!

We will also look at practicing, potential, goal setting, taking action, evolution, tone, instruments, effects, techniques, grooving, rhythm, dynamics, harmony, scales, chords, listening, styles, and patience. There will be sections for you to fill out personal thoughts and ideas, come up with new ways of playing, and examine your perceived strengths and weaknesses. This is all part of the creative process.

Audio

In each chapter there is a CD accompaniment with a metronome or drums. There will be a bass idea on each example and then its backing track. The corresponding track number for each example or song is listed with the audio icon. TRACK 1

CHAPTER 1

Creativity

Create: to cause to come into existence, bring into being, make and originate.

Whoever you are, whatever you do regardless of your background, you have creative thoughts. As a musician you hear things in your mind and when action is applied to your thoughts, you cause to exist. Just like the melodies you've heard all your life. If asked to recreate a melody like "Mary Had a Little Lamb" (or any familiar song) you would, at the very least, have a sense of what it sounds like even if your musical abilities are limited.

This creative process opens up your creative "sense." Being open is letting your creativity flow without question, to allow and make space for it to come through. Being creative is about being able to focus your attention on what you've created long enough to set it in motion.

Thought

Thoughts are mental pictures in your mind. We all have thoughts and sometimes, to our detriment, we think far too much. Without thought, the mind would not form the pictures from which to create. In music, it is the sense of hearing which occupies that space in your mind.

When dealing with music, thoughts can be your best friend or worst enemy. All form must manifest first in the mind by your thoughts/senses. If you hear a musical idea in your head, to let it out you must concentrate and allow it to manifest. This is where it can be your best friend. If you put action behind it, you can bring it into creation.

As a worst enemy, a creative thought comes in and, instead of acting on it or allowing it, the mind's old beliefs come in and pinch it off with other thoughts. Thoughts like, "You don't have time. Will others like this? Who do you think you are? This is not good enough," and so on. This line of thought blocks the process of creativity. This distraction arises and you either move past it and continue, or it is too great and you quit the task. You need to be able to focus the mind enough so that these distractions do not get in the way of what you choose to accomplish. Great creative minds have the ability to focus their attention, to focus their thoughts like a laser beam, on what they want. For some, this happens naturally. For the rest of us, we need to practice concentration. The great thing about this is, just like anything else, the brain can be trained and thoughts can be focused.

To demonstrate this concept, try writing with your non-dominant hand. I'm serious, try it. It's pretty difficult since you've been writing with your other hand since childhood. If you spent enough time writing with the other hand, in time you'd write quite well. If you have never focused your thoughts, making attempts to focus may take some time, but it is attainable. If you think in short spurts this is fine, also. This makes us unique because, not all minds think alike.

The key to productive thinking is keeping the mind on what you want. This is the focus of the creative process. Have you ever "lost time" creating or doing something? When does whatever you're doing seem to come naturally? The creative flow comes when you're not thinking about anything except the task at hand.

Another thought on thoughts. When creating, the mind is needed to execute the appointed task, not to think about the past or future. This is the distraction from the moment you are in. If you want to know where someone's thoughts are, look at their results! What are your results?

Action

This is the process, or state, of being active. This is not being distracted, this is doing. Having the courage to dare and the faith to finish what you start. Most people have an idea of what they want, they think it will never be "good enough," so it never gets done. They get distracted by their thoughts and forget about doing for the **joy of doing**. Success in this area is about, "it's not what you do but how you do it." Why is it that so many amateurs succeed in music and seasoned professionals don't? How is it that two similar businesses can open up in the same city, and while one thrives, the other one dies? It is based on their process of doing. Look at their results and you will see where their thoughts are. Thoughts without action are just thoughts. Thoughts with action are creation. What I'm driving at here is, to create no matter what.

What's in the Way?

Now, I'll ask you to take some action around awareness. I want you to become aware of what you think and what might be blocking your creative flow.

Do some writing around your thoughts. Here are a few ideas:

1. Log all your thoughts for a half an hour. Write everything that enters your mind. What did you learn about your thoughts? Are you surprised?
2. Next time you sit down with your bass, pay attention to all the thoughts that enter your mind. What are they? Are they negative or positive? Write them down. How often are you distracted?
3. Take note of how many times you think about playing your bass but don't get around to it.

These ideas allow you to know how to get past these thoughts for the next time. Arm yourself with awareness so you can control the actions you want to put forth, instead of allowing thoughts and old beliefs to keep you distracted. It never helps to get mad or beat yourself up. Just realize how you react. Take off the auto-pilot and get in the driver's seat. Remember, if you write with your opposite hand everyday, it will soon become as fluid as your dominant hand. Welcome this new challenge of growing and changing as a creative musician.

Patience

We are in a "microwave world" where everyone wants results now. This impatient attitude creates severe obstacles when a bassist who doesn't have a solid foundation needs to expand. The lack of patience when working on a new method can make or break it. If you're patient, you'll get to the other side. I often hear, "I don't have the time," but anyone can **make** the time when needed. Anyone who wants something bad enough makes the time and finds a way. Life is how you perceive it to be. The one thing I've seen in true successful musicians over the years is the ability to approach any situation, no matter how busy it is, and focus. Creation is not a race, so be patient with yourself and its process. Most people will be on the verge of breaking through to a new technique, a new song idea, a great new bass line or new method, but then get distracted and back down. See things through to the end. Sometimes sitting through with patience feels like breaking the sound barrier; it's uncomfortable until you reach the correct speed then it is smooth and easy.

What Do You Want?

Apparently, most people are unaware of what they truly desire. Ask most people what they want and they tell you what they don't want. When creating, look at what you want and what you like. If you approach things with a positive and open perception, you are more willing to hear a new idea and create something unique. If your mind is focused on what you don't like, you'll be too busy complaining and making excuses about your inability to play the perfect bass part. You'll be feeling too cluttered and bad to try different ways to play or write. You'll be impatient and frustrated versus open and willing. Think about this on a purely psychological level: thinking good equals feeling good.

In your brain, you have something called the Reticular Activating System. It is a filter system that looks for proof about judgments your subconscious makes. If you think that "this is hard," the Reticular Activating System (RAS) looks for the proof that supports this belief. Same goes if you think, "this is easy." The RAS responds to what you feed it. Look at all the results of successful people. They have the vision of what they want and the will to see it through. It's not about how good you are, it's about how you do it. (There have been volumes written on the RAS by scientists, so if you'd like to look into it further, get on the web or visit your local library.)

Goal Setting

Know what you want and then, whenever you pick up your bass, focus on that. Set big and small goals around whatever you want. If you are excited about practice, you'll practice. If you're excited about creating a bass line, you'll find the motivation. Setting goals is a great motivator and barometer for your playing. Before you sit down to create, set a goal, now matter how small, and stick to it. Without this step, you could just aimlessly practice without vision that wastes your valuable time. Isn't it obvious that if you spend the time to focus, create, and see it through with action, you'll improve and grow by leaps and bounds? What are your goals? What smaller goals can you write down to help you achieve the bigger goals that are consistent with your vision? What are your long-term musical goals? List five.

Mind & Emotions

I'm sure you've heard of players that don't like learning theory because it will hinder their emotions while playing. By the same token, you've heard others mention players who sound academic. I'm here to say that this is bull sh@#! Music is an art form. Judging art is like saying what is good or bad about chicken: everyone has an opinion. If one believes that learning music theory will hinder their emotion, it will. If you think you play with feeling, you do, and no amount of theory will take that away unless you **choose to believe it**. The same goes for those who learn the academics of music and judge players who don't as being lesser. Right-brained people are attracted to right-brain methods and left-brain people are, in the same way, attracted to the like. It is each person's responsibility to decide on what methods work best for them. What I'm driving at here is for you to be open to all forms of expression. Learn and grow because being armed with knowledge and expressive with emotion is why most play music in the first place. Head and heart can go hand in hand. In this book, I'll ask you to practice both. Sometimes it is a head decision that sparks a creative thought and a feeling that sparks an idea you need theory to finish!

Wrap Up

Now that you've made it this far, we'll dig into playing some bass. The goal of this introduction has been for you to become aware of how your thinking impacts your playing. This book is about creativity first and bass second. You get out what you put into this book, so I invite you to work through the entire book and skip nothing.

CHAPTER 2

Practicing

Practicing music is like practicing sports. You have to put in time to get excellent results! The reason you play a sport is for enjoyment and/or passion (if it's a passion, it satisfies your emotions which makes it feel fun). To excel in the game, you have to practice different aspects of it. Similarly, to enjoy and excel at bass, you will need to practice different aspects of the instrument to be well-rounded. If you want results you have to put quality focus into your practice time. If you don't, your weak spots might hinder your advancement. If your effort is half-hearted, your playing will sound that way. Just so you know, short attentive spurts can be more effective than long sessions where your mind wanders. Being efficient is about focus, not time.

Types of Practice

1. *Technical:* The ablity to move your fingers over the strings of an instrument to play particular notes. The more proficient you are at finger techniques, the more freely you will be able to express your musical ideas.
2. *Mental:* Learning how to put notes, scales, theory, and concepts together. The more you know mentally and practice without your instrument, the easier it becomes to act and react or know what to do when new situations arise.
3. *Auditory:* Listening to music and developing a "good ear" is essential to becoming a great bass player. This might be hearing intervals and chord changes, understanding and hearing rhythm, or listening to music and learning how to write down what you hear. Trained listening enables you to express yourself and play music in its purest form, because hearing is how music is translated.
4. *Rhythmic:* Having a natural "feel" or groove. Having a sense of time and/or being able to interpret time as rhythm or time signatures.
5. *Performance:* Putting it all together. The technical, mental, rhythmic, and auditory in an immediate setting. From practicing sightreading and improvisation to jamming just for fun, you will need to link everything together to create great music.

Results

Each individual has different areas or talents when it comes to playing bass. Some are naturally gifted at techniques, others have great ears, some have a great memory and learn theory and scales, and others have a natural instinct for the groove and feel. If you were to look at your natural abilities, what areas would you be the best at? The technical, mental, auditory, rhythmic, or performance?

Now I want you to list the order of your abilities from strongest to weakest. If your answer is "I don't know," ask a teacher or musical peer. This is really important to getting results, so be honest with yourself.

Strengths: Technical, Mental, Auditory, Rhythmic, and Performance

1.	
2.	
3.	
4.	
5.	

On a scale of 1 to 10, rate yourself in each area. 10 being of masterful ability and 1 being at complete novice. In the next column, record your musical goals. Some may want to be a 10 in technical while others only desire intermediate abilities overall.

Ability	Are Now	Want To Be
Technical		
Mental		
Auditory		
Rhythmic		
Playing		

Now on a scale of 1 to 5, rate how much fun you have in each area. 5 is exceeding joy and 1 is complete disinterest.

Enjoyment	
Technical	
Mental	
Auditory	
Rhythmic	
Playing	

Now you have an idea about what you excel in, what areas you may want to improve on, and what you enjoy practicing. This part is to encourage you. This isn't about comparing, but identifying where your abilities are and where you want to be.

Getting results comes from looking at the data (your information) and applying action to what you want to achieve. If you are low in technical ability and want to be a 10, this is an area to focus the majority of your practice time. If you want to be a well-rounded player, look at the areas you are low in and spend time on those first. Now is the time to make choices when you practice. You have a choice to practice what comes easy or areas that are more challenging. There are no set rules; it's all up to you.

I've found that most players will tend to spend the most time on their strengths. This method can leave major gaps in their playing. Perhaps other areas aren't as fun to practice. We are going to look at this so you can help to make those areas more fun and workable. Music can be a job or hobby, and it can bring joy or frustration. The focus is for you to enjoy the entire process, get the most out of yourself, and create great bass lines.

Creative Warm-Up Practice

Now that you are armed with the knowledge of what your goals are, what you are good at, and what areas you wish to improve on (you did the exercises right?), you should have a good idea of what you want. Here, we are going to look at several ways to make practice creative and ever-evolving. But first, let's tune up.

Tune Up

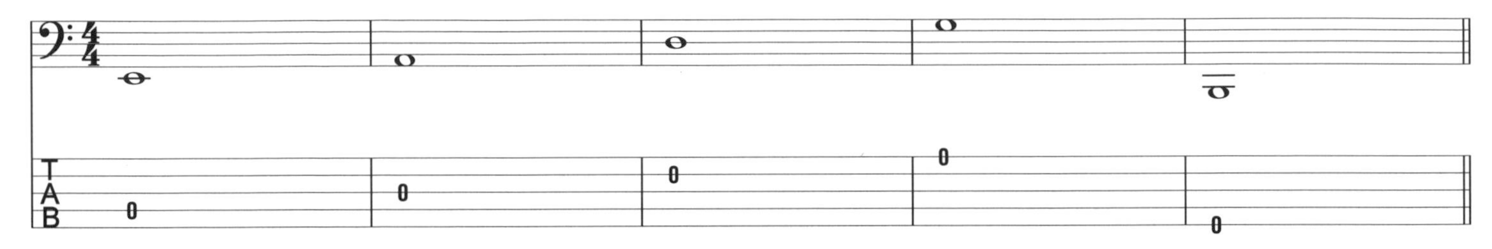

Warming Up

No one has ever said that warming up isn't creative! Let's take a simple warm-up technique, then vary it five ways with either notes or rhythm. When we are done, you can come up with five more to create ten new warm ups.

Warm Up Original

Variation 1

Variation 2

Variation 3

Variation 4

Variation 5

Now it is your turn; write out five more variations of the original warm up.

Variation 6

T
A
B

Variation 7

T
A
B

Variation 8

T
A
B

Variation 9

T
A
B

Variation 10

T
A
B

See how easy that was? If it was challenging for you, stop trying to do it "right" and just put something down. Don't over analyze. Try to use just patterns and rhythms to make variations. What about different techniques like hammer-ons or slap-bass technique? What if you concentrated on your plucking hand instead of your fretting hand? There are endless possibilities.

Creative Metronome Practice

Practicing with a metronome helps us acclimate to time. We are human, so without a reference, we can speed up or slow down without knowing it. Having internal timing, as close as possible to actual time, is a huge blessing. The good thing about timing is it can be learned. A bass player's job is to keep good time, so work regularly with a metronome or drummer to internally feel this external clock. Having great time in music is like having a great time in life, where you are in the right place at the right time!

A metronome is set in relation to the current time signature. This means that, at 100 beats per minute (BPM) in 4/4 time, four clicks equal one measure (four quarter notes per measure = 4/4 time). In this section, we'll break down how a metronome can be set different ways. Here's an example of a metronome set to different meters. On the CD, each one plays four times.

4/4 time equals 4 quarter notes at 72 BPM

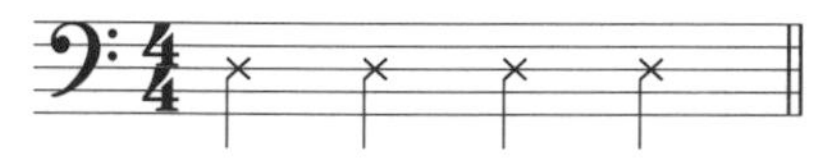

3/4 time equals 3 quarter notes at 90 BPM

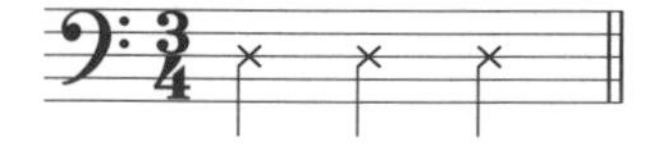

6/8 time equals 6 eighth notes at 165 BPM

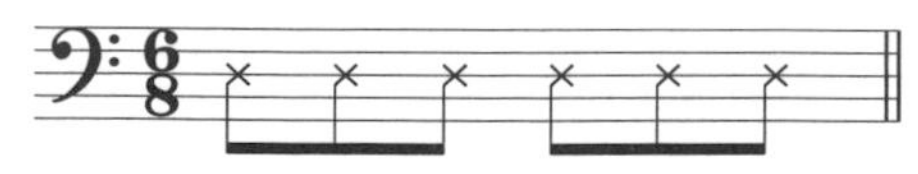

7/4 time equals 7 quarter notes at 122 BPM

Now let's get creative. I guarantee your timing will improve when trying these methods. Usually, a metronome is set to one click per beat. We'll start each example as such, then modify it. On tracks 6–9 I'll play the written bass part for the first half of the audio example. After a count-off it will be your turn!

Double Time

Sometimes when a tempo is really slow, you can make the music easier to follow by setting the click to double time. For this example, the tempo is at 52 BPM, so set the metronome to 104 BPM. *(Editor's note: at this setting, the clicks are eighth notes rather than quarter notes).*

Half Time (clicks on beats 1 and 3)

The tempo is 140, so we set the metronome to 70.

Half Time (clicks on beats 2 and 4)

Same concept but a little trickier for some. This is great when practicing swing music or walking bass lines. This example is played with a shuffle feel. See Chapter 6 for more on the shuffle feel.

♩ = 120 (1st & 2nd time)
𝅗𝅥 = 60 (3rd & 4th time, with Half-time feel)

G

Play 8 times

T A B: 3 2 3 3 5 | 5 4 4 2 5

Set for one click per measure only. This is really great for testing your timing, especially when you slow the tempo down. This can be set on beats 1, 2, 3, or 4.

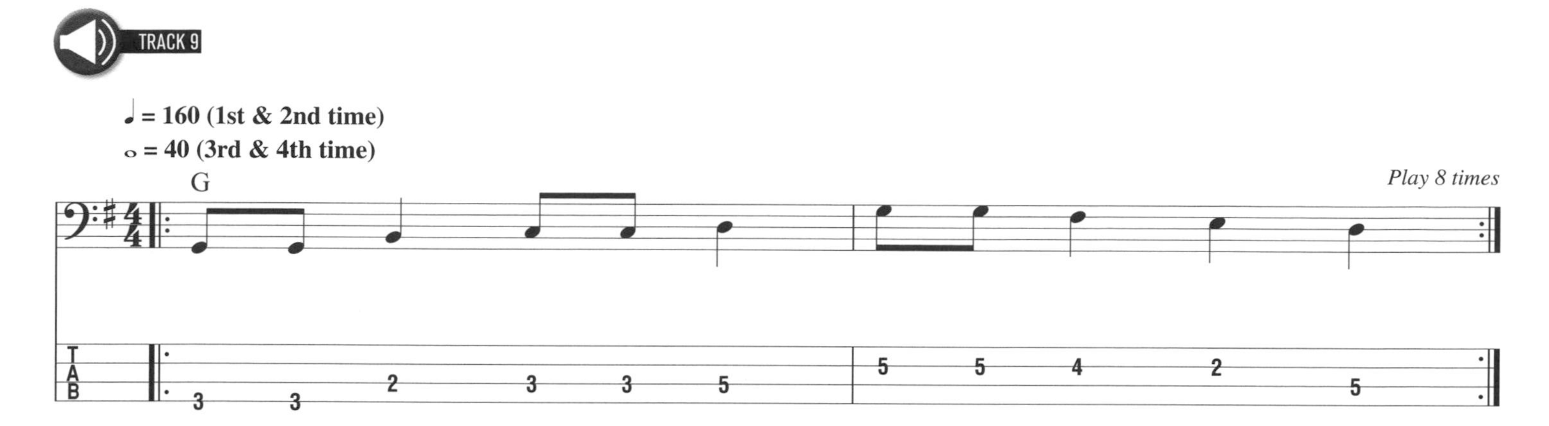

Essentially, what we have done is kept the tempo constant while shifting the metronome to fall on different beats. This is a great way to mix up practicing and add some difficulty.

Areas of Music

Remember the fives types of practice? This is the same concept but quite a few steps deeper into creative expression. Creativity is sparked by the approach. If someone gives you a song idea and you can't come up with something, you can draw on the types of practice or areas of music to come up with an idea. You can approach a piece of music or a musical idea given to you in a technical, mental, auditory, or rhythmic manner or by playing and seeing what happens. If one area does not seem to work out, you can approach it from any of the other areas.

In a technical approach, maybe palm muting, slapping, or hammer-ons will spark an idea. With a mental approach, you can look at the key or chords of the song and try different notes from the chords being played. If you tried the auditory method, you could listen to some music that's similar and see what others do. This is like the saying, "good artists borrow, great artists steal." Maybe when you interpret a stolen idea, it yields something you would have never tried and, in the end, doesn't sound like it's borrowed at all. With a rhythm approach, try tapping/slapping/striking the strings till you find a rhythm that you like. Also, use a drummer as a springboard to decide how to play.

Let's take a few ideas and build on them using this method to create. We will elaborate on these areas more later in the book.

In this next example, I will create five different bass lines coming from all the areas: technical, mental, auditory, rhythmic, and performance. On track 10, each example flows right into the next. There are endless possibilities. After you hear my parts, come up with your own from each area to see what comes out.

This is a basic rock beat with two measures each of Am and Dm:

Technical – I played this one with a slap and pop technique that locks in with the kick drum. See more on slap and pop in Chapter 4.

Mental – I outlined the chords using root, third, and fifth, while locking in with the kick.

Auditory – I listened to a few bass lines that I thought may sound cool and adapted to our groove. This sparked a completely new idea.

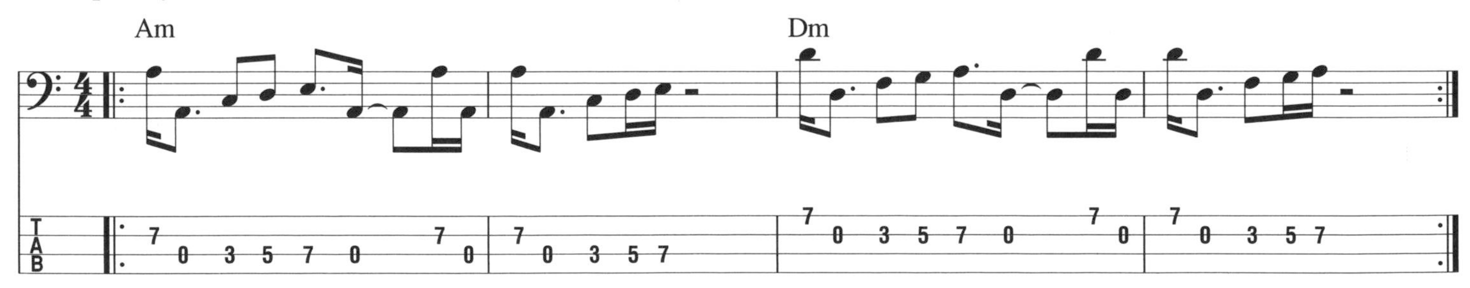

Rhythmic – I tried some different rhythms around the drum part.

Performance – I went for a more melodic and long-note approach.

As you can hear, I came up with several parts that varied greatly. It took less than ten minutes to come up with these five parts. It even took me longer to write them out than it did to create them.

You try it! I'll loop this track eight times.

Stretch Yourself

Stretch yourself by trying new ways of being open-minded. Creativity flows where attention goes. If your attention is on giving up, that is what you'll do. If you are excited and open to trying something that is new or difficult, chances are your creativity will come forth.

Don't be critical of yourself either. The more you try, the more ideas will come through. Here is an exercise to try when working on being creative. This is called a *stretch,* where you move out of your comfort zone. Once a week on the same day, write down a new stretch. It has to be something you wouldn't normally do, yet is attainable. If you don't do it, let it go and start anew the following week. It's not about feeling bad if you don't do it, it's about intending to do something. Try working with a fellow musician on the same day so you'll be held accountable.

The rule for stretching is that it has to be definable. If you told me what it was, I could tell if you did it or not. A stretch like, "I'll practice more," is not acceptable. I don't know what your regular schedule is! It needs to be something measurable like, "I'll practice a half hour a day for five days this week." Or, "I'll spend two hours this week writing new music." The important thing is to set yourself up for success.

CHAPTER 3

Tone

In this chapter we will be discussing *tone. Tone* is defined as the sound and quality of a note. When we discuss tone in reference to the bass, there are many factors that create each individual characteristic of its tone. The word *timbre* comes to mind.

Timbre

Timbre would be a more definite term for tone because it distinguishes between types of sound production from different musical instruments. For example, a Fender Precision bass and a Fender Jazz bass have two distinctly different timbres, just like an acoustic or upright bass sounds much different than an electric bass. When factoring in strings, amps, effects, bass model, and wood types, there are infinite choices to expand our creative palate—either for tone's sake or to spark creativity. This is why session bassists use different basses to give a producer or artist more sonic options. In this chapter, we will break down what kind of tones you can create and the effect it has.

Basses

What is the right bass for you? I can't answer that question, but I can give you some tips so you can find what you are looking for. First and foremost, I have to say a person's physical make up (bones, skin, and fingers) has as much to do with tone as anything else. This is why people who try to copy a specific artist don't emulate them exactly. Your hands are much like a singer's voice. Let yourself be you and no one else. It's great to have influences and like other bass player's tones, but don't forget who you are.

There are so many basses on the market today it can be overwhelming. Different brands, active or passive electronics, and models with four, five, six or even seven strings! The best advice I have is to find a bass that is comfortable and sounds good. Your favorite player's bass might not fit what you are looking for, but it's a start. The playability of these instruments is a matter of personal taste and tone. A few great current bass brands are Stuart Spector Design, Modulus, Roscoe, Ibanez, Fender, and DP Custom.

For me, picking up a different bass adjusts my creative approach, whether the bass feels or sounds different. In particular, grabbing a fretless can help my creative process.

Spector

Roscoe

DP Custom

Woods

The main part that actually gives a bass its tone is the body's wood. If you know what kind of tone the body wood generates, you'll be headed in the right direction. Other factors arise when different combinations of neck woods, fingerboards, and laminates of more exotic woods come into play. However, the body of a specific wood carries a particular tone. As a rule, the heavier the wood, the more the sustain. Alder and swamp ash are great body woods that are in the middle as far as weight and great tone.

Pickups

Pickups transfer string vibrations into an electrical signal. Most pickups are magnetic because they use a magnet to "pick up" the vibration of metal strings. Piezoelectric pickups use a transducer crystal to convert the string vibrations so nylon strings can be used. Newer technologies, such as lasers, are also used.

On most basses, magnetic pickups are used and different types of magnets lend themselves to different sounds. Two common pickups are the P-Bass pickup (as in Precision Bass) and the J-Bass pickup (as in Jazz Bass). These are both single-coil pickups. Soapbar pickups (which resemble a bar of soap) are often used as well. These can be a P, J, or a humbucking pickup (which consists of two coils).

Placement of the pickup greatly affects the sound. Pickups near the neck sound warmer (bigger) and a pickup near the bridge is brighter (tighter). Bass pickups also have volume controls, blend, pan controls, bass, treble, and/or midrange controls. This depends on the model and adjusting these controls can greatly change the tone.

P-Bass Pickup

J-Bass Pickup

Soapbar Pickup

from left: SMB-4a, SMB-5a

Humbucking Pickup

Amplifiers & Speaker Cabinets

Just like basses, there is a massive amount of bass amplifiers on the market. Again, consider what the players or artists whom you admire use and go from there. You can buy a *combo amp* that is an amp and speaker all in one. You can also buy amplifiers and cabinets separately. These are more versatile by allowing higher wattage or tone combinations. Amplifiers also come with a variety of options. Among the possibilities are tube, solid state, tube and solid state combinations, parametric or graphic equalizations, various built-in effects, and different wattage options.

Mark Bass

Tube amplifiers give you a warmer tone overall, but they tend to weigh a bit more. Also, tubes require replacement every few years. This can be worth dealing with to get the warm tone tube amps produce. Solid-state amplifiers have a crisper, brighter tone and can be packed into a smaller, more lightweight box.

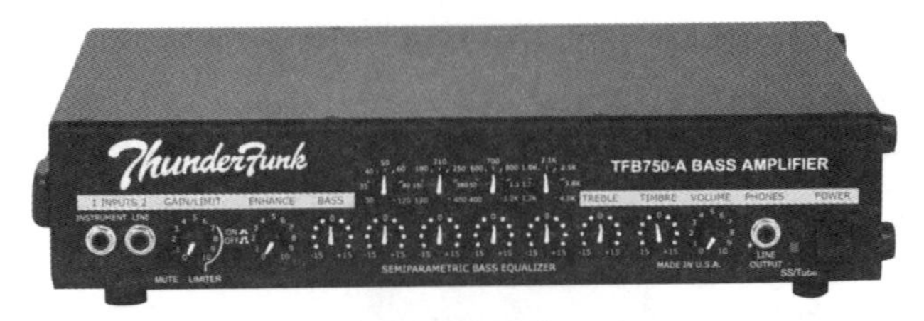

Thunder Funk

Combinations of tube and solid-state amps have a tube preamp section and a solid-state power section (run by a circuit board). This gives you the best of both worlds: the warmth of tubes and the brightness of solid state. These amps also make for a lighter, more compact setup. Power handling, or wattage, depends on where you play and how loud you need to be. For a small setting, 100 to 300 watts are adequate. For louder needs, 350 to 1,200 watt amps will be more than adequate.

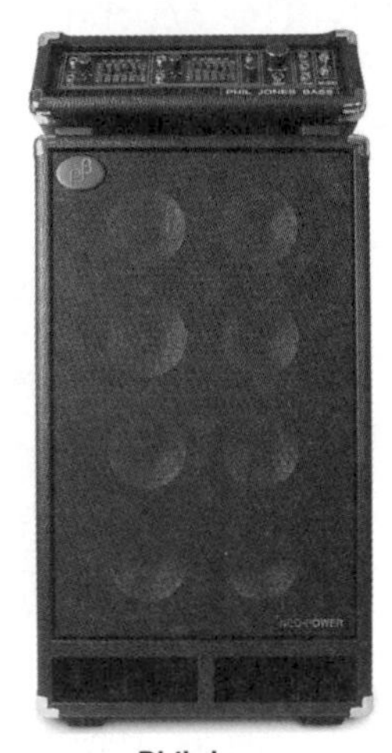
Phil Jones

Speaker cabinets have come a long way in the past few years. They are much more compact, versatile, and able to handle higher wattage than ever before. Speaker cabinets come in a wide variety of speaker combinations, from 1x12, 2x10, 2x12, 1x15, 1x18, 4x10, to 8x8 inch speakers! Most cabinets have a horn or tweeter to help produce crisper highs.

When deciding on what you need, try out several brands, consider your budget, and open your ears to decide what sounds good to you. Several brands specializing in bass amplification are Euphonic Audio, Mark Bass, SWR, Galien Krueger, Hartke, Agular, Thunder Funk, Ampeg, and Phil Jones Bass. Don't forget Peavey and Fender who not only make bass cabinets, but PA gear and musical instruments as well.

Ampeg

Strings

There are three main string types for electric bass and what you use is a matter of personal preference. There are roundwound, flatwound, and groundwound (sometimes called halfwound). The main differences are in the string's sound and texture.

Roundwound strings

These are the most commonly used strings. They are made by wrapping a steel, or nylon, core with a continuous length of round wire made of nickel or stainless steel. Roundwound strings have a bright, crisp sound and good volume.

Flatwound strings

These strings are smooth and made in a similar way as roundwound. In this case, the wrappings are made of flat metal tape or ribbon. This results in a much duller or mellower tone compared to the roundwounds.

Groundwound strings

This is a hybrid string that combines flatwound and roundwound strings. They are made the same way as roundwound, but the winding is ground down and polished. Groundwound strings, as you might guess, sound somewhere in between the other two string types.

As stated before, strings are a matter of taste. Try out all three types and see which of them best fits your needs and sound. Each string type can change the way you play. When I have flatwound strings on or if my roundwounds are old, their tones inspire me to play a little differently.

Stainless Steel or Nickelwound

If you choose to go with roundwounds for your bass, another option to consider is whether to use stainless steel or nickel strings. Stainless steel sound brighter and usually last longer. Nickel is a softer material that will wear less on your frets and have a nice warm tone. Again, it's a matter of personal preference.

Pick or Fingers

With regards to your pick-hand technique, having the ability to play any way you choose to achieve a desired tone is the goal. Sometimes fingers are in order and sometimes a pick might be the perfect approach.

I improvised this part with my fingers on the first two times through, then I switched to a pick. Notice how the tone changes. Try it yourself with track 13.

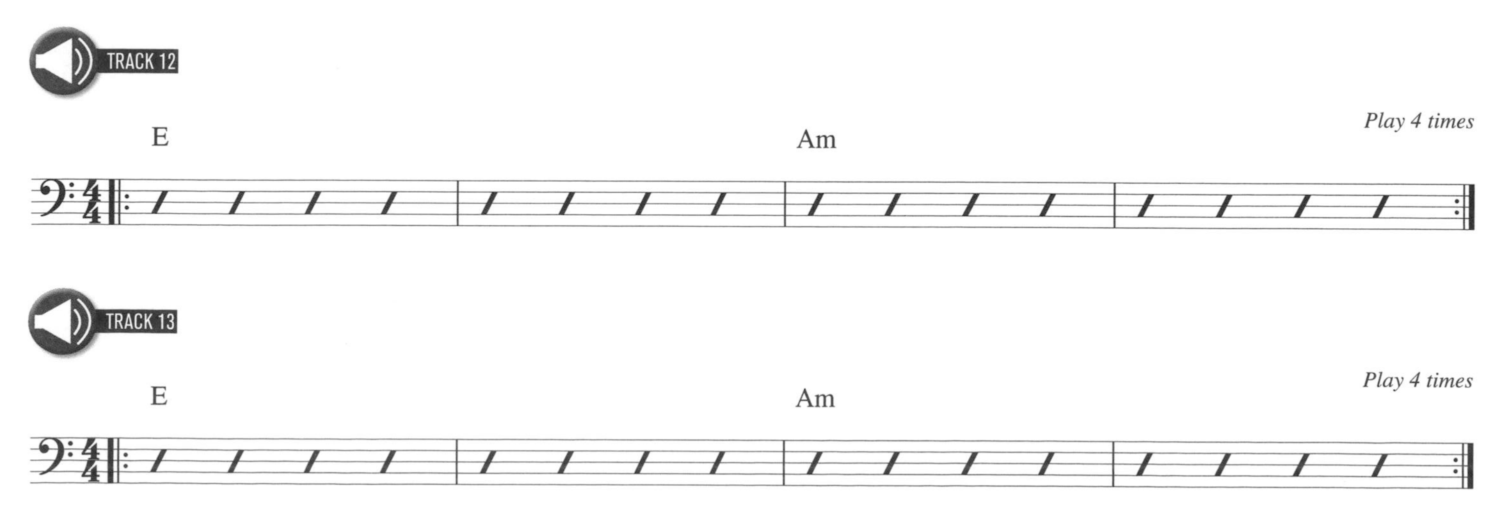

Different approaches can help inspire a new idea or change a part you are dissatisfied with.

Plucking Location

Another way to create different tone is by where you pluck the string itself. When you pluck close to the bridge, your tone is sharper and more distinct. Plucking closer to the neck rounds out your tone for a warmer, less distinct sound. For instance, when playing a slow ballad you may want to pluck closer to the neck to achieve a bigger sound. When playing a solo, try plucking closer to the bridge so your notes stick out more.

Effects & Equalization

Effects are great tools to color your tone and *equalization* (EQ) is used to change the frequency of your sound. Trying different tones may help you play differently than you would before. Great players like Bootsy Collins and Justin Medlin Johnson have used effects to come up with some pretty interesting sounds that take bass outside the standard tone and role. Tone can inspire, change a part, or bring a song to life.

In this section, we'll go through some examples of where certain effects can be added to enhance a part, or EQ tricks can bring a bass out in the mix. This serves as a brief overview with the purpose of enhancing or helping your creativity. It is not to teach you about effect parameters and the sound spectrum of human hearing. The effects we will work with are distortion, overdrive (fuzz), chorus, octave, envelope filters, phaser (flange), delay, and compression.

Halfway through each example is a count-off for you to try the example yourself, or create a completely new bass part or effect.

Distortion, Overdrive, and Fuzz

Distortion, overdrive, and fuzz involve the clipping of a sound to produce distortion. On a scale, overdrive includes the least amount of clipping and distortion (fuzz) has the most. It's a great sound, especially to fill out more space or make your sound heavier. I'll use all three sounds in this musical example.

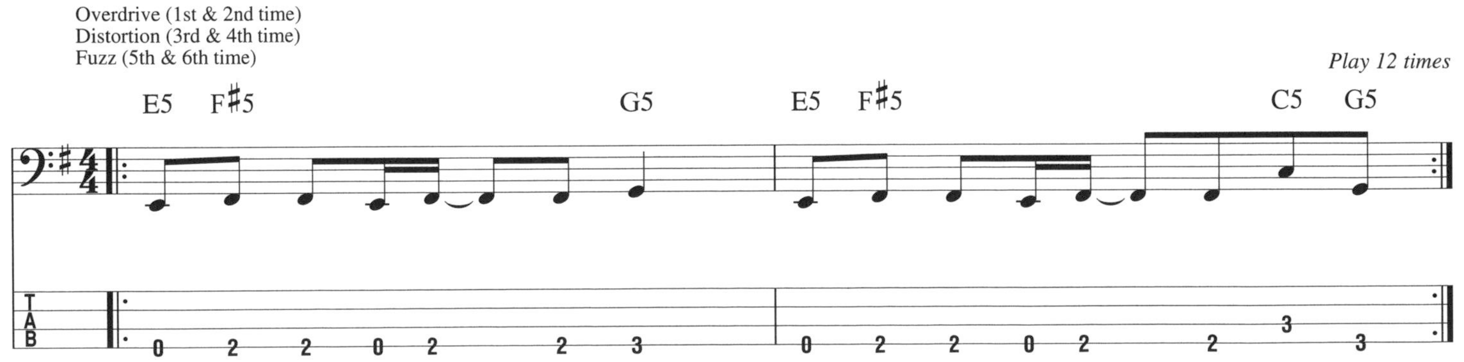

Chorus

A chorus blends your tone with a modulated copy. This creates a shimmering effect similar to a fretless bass. It's especially great when holding long notes.

Octave or Pitch Shifter

The octave effect is just that. It takes your signal and produces a double an octave below or above. Pitch shifting is similar but adds a pre-determined interval (other than an octave) to the original pitch. I'll use an octaver on the example.

Envelope Filters

Envelope filters are essentially an effect that changes your sound by cutting certain frequencies. The amount of control this effect has depends on the type. Some are triggered by dynamics, foot movement (as in a wah-wah), while others are controlled by buttons to change the rate. The auto-wah in this next example is great for funky bass parts.

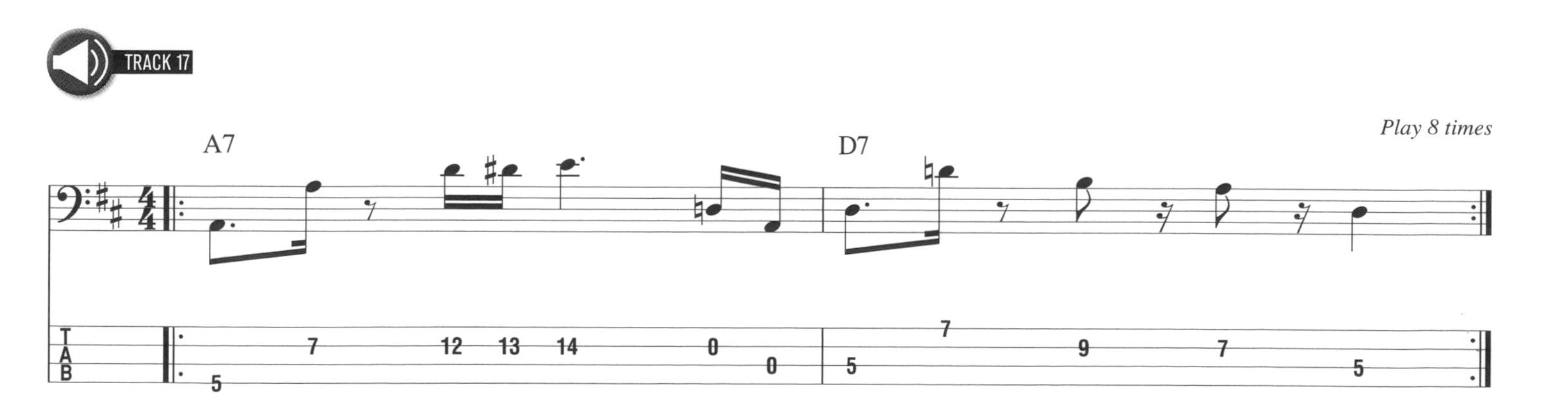

Flange

Flange is a time-based effect that mixes two identical sounds and delays the time in small and gradual amounts. This creates a sweeping comp-like effect.

Delay

Delay takes your signal, copies it, and reproduces it at a later moment than the initial attack.

Compression

Compression is more like a balancer. It makes loud notes softer and soft notes louder. I'll use it here in a slap and pop example so that you can hear the part balance out more evenly. I'll play without compression first, then add it so you can hear the difference. Check out more on the slap and pop technique in Chapter 4.

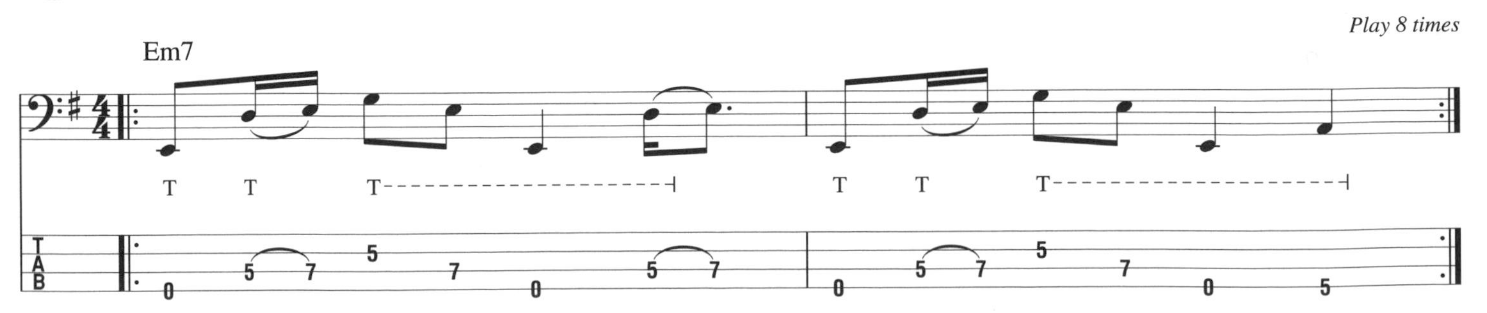

Equalization

Equalization changes the frequency envelope of a sound. It can make or break your tone by adding a unique flavor to a bass part. What I'll do in this example is start with a flat bass signal, then subtract frequencies as the example plays starting from low to high. Then, I'll add some particular frequencies to change the complete character of the sound.

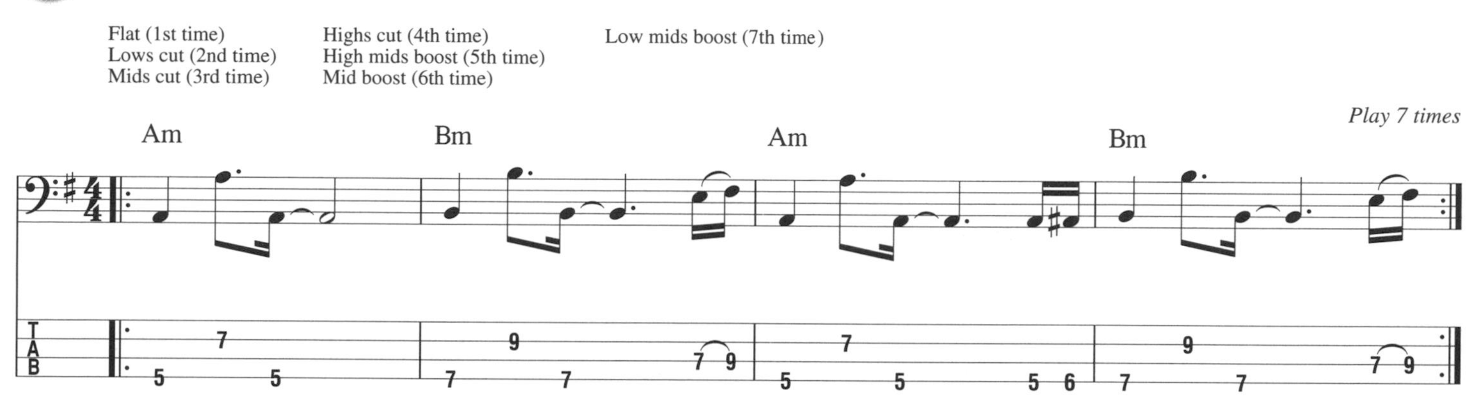

Note Location

Another thing to be aware of is the location of notes you play and the different timbre that results. For example, an open A sounds different than an A on the E string. They are the same note but, due to the instrument, open strings sound different than a fretted note. Another case is how the C note on the A string sounds a little different than the C on the E string. This is because the E string has a heavier and rounder timbre while the C on the A string has more clarity. Even the process of moving from string to string versus playing all the notes on one string changes your approach and creates subtle articulation nuances.

Octave Range

A great way to change up a part, or build it, is by using octaves. Playing a part up or down an octave creates a different sound. Following are some helpful tips on this subject.

Use different octave ranges to build a part. During different sections or transitions, play the same part an octave lower or higher. In measures 1–6, the same part is played in three different octaves. After you create a part, add excitement by playing it an octave higher right before you transition. In measures 7–14, it is the same part played many different ways using the same notes in the same order. This is a great example of the many possibilities to spice up or create a unique flow. It's simple but effective. At the repeat, the bass drops out so you can play.

TRACK 22

Working with tone, using effects, grabbing a different bass, trying a new amp, or messing with EQ settings helps to spark creative ideas. It's also a great excuse to buy new gear!

CHAPTER 4

Technique

There are many ways to approach playing an instrument. In this chapter, we'll look at some common and not so common ways to technically approach the bass. Sometimes the most simple approach, like playing a note long or short, can make or break the part. Other times, using a new or different technique inspires an idea that creates the perfect bass line.

Staccato & Legato

The duration of a note can have a huge effect on the groove. Deciding to play a note long or short can change the entire idea. *Staccato* is to cut notes short and *legato* is to play each note for its full duration. Also, whether you pluck every note for a staccato feel or strive for legato phrasing by use of hammer-ons or pull-offs, either one can bring you to new creative territory.

Playing staccato is indicated by a dot under or above a notehead. This is used for easier reading, otherwise rhythms would be written with a bunch of rests. Playing staccato leaves space in between notes allowing everything else to stick out. It also adds a rhythmic quality to the bass and drum parts.

You will know to play legato if there is a short line under the note. Sonically, playing long, full notes lays down a solid foundation for the drum part.

The key to tasteful playing is interpretation of knowing when and where to play a short or long note. You may already do this instinctively, but this concept may still be totally foreign to you. The first step is awareness and execution. Let's play some exercises using staccato and legato lines.

The first example is an eighth-note rock groove played without embellishments. As we add staccato notes to the line, the entire groove changes.

TRACK 23
E
B
F♯m
A
E
B
F♯m
A
E
B
F♯m
A

Try the same progression using various combinations of staccato notes to see what you can come up with.

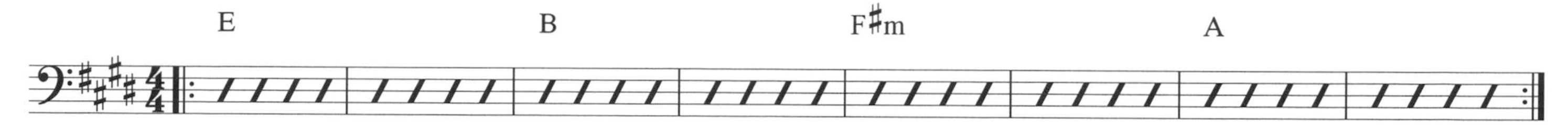

Now we'll play a bass line incorporating octaves. First I'll play the part as written two times through, then I'll add more legato by letting the octaves ring together. After that, the bass drops out so you can try.

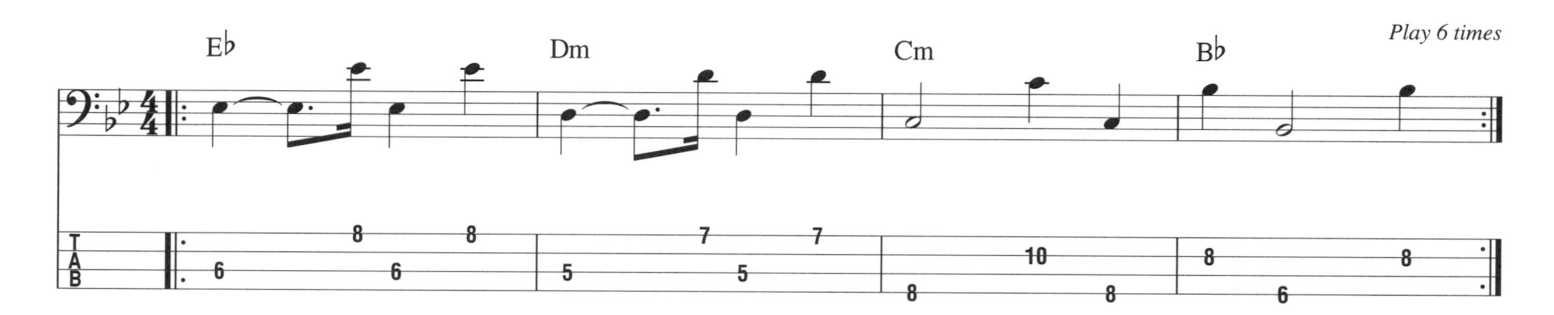

Hammer-ons & Pull-offs

Using *hammer-ons* and *pull-offs* adds a flowing, legato sound to a part while plucking every note tends to be a more staccato sound. Let's take a look at this legato approach.

To play a *hammer-on*, place one of your fingers on a fret and pluck the note. While that note is ringing, hammer on to a higher note in pitch. The force of the hammer-on causes another note to ring without plucking again. To play a *pull-off*, you place two of your fingers on different frets on the same string and pluck that string. While the note is ringing, pull off with that finger to the lower note. The force of the pull-off causes another note to ring without re-attacking.

In the next example, we'll play a bass line using a legato approach, then switch to plucking every note so you can hear the difference. Next, I'll combine the techniques and play the notes longer and shorter for you to see that, just by approach, how a bass line can sound different.

The chord changes are written above the bass part so you can come up with your own parts for the following track.

TRACK 26
A7
Gm7
let ring
TRACK 27
Play 4 times

Dead Notes

Dead, or muted, notes are a great way to enhance your sound. They move air and add a rhythmic aspect to a line without filling harmonic space. The key to making dead notes effective is to play them dynamically louder. They are notated by an X on the staff and tablature.

Here's an example with the dead note located on a lower-pitched string, the same string, then on a higher string. Even though the dead note has no pitch, the heavier strings have a different timbre than the higher strings when using dead notes. Try it out on track 29.

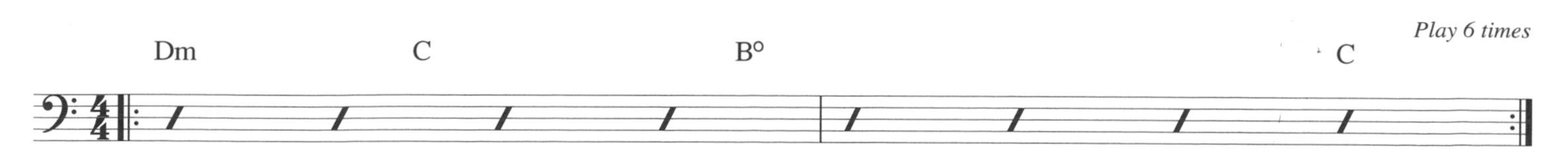

Palm Muting

Palm muting is a guitar technique used to mute the strings with the palm of your plucking hand. Whether you play bass with a pick or fingers, this is a great technique to change the timbre of your bass and give it a nice staccato tone. Rest the palm of your plucking hand on the bridge of your bass and strike the strings. To change the tone, move your palm toward the neck if you want a deader sound and move it on the bridge itself for the notes to ring out. This technique is great for verse sections, when the dynamics become quiet, or to change up your sound.

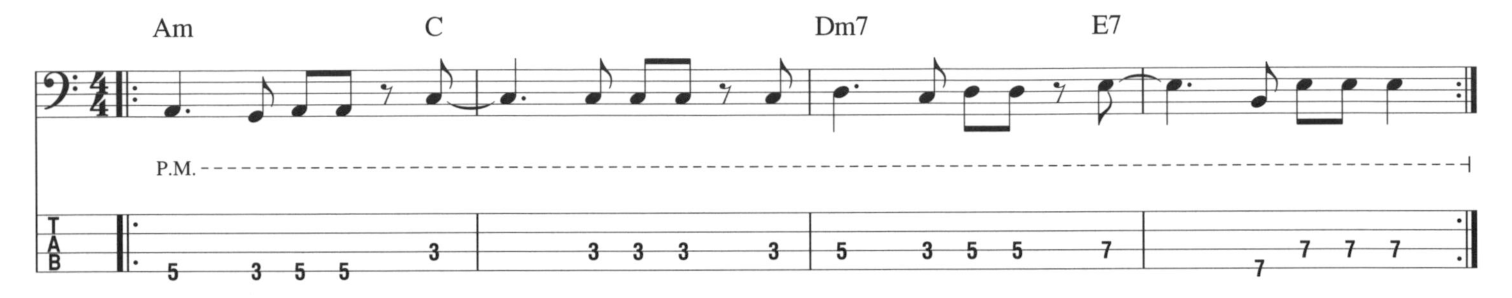

Now try palm muting and see what you can come up with over these chords.

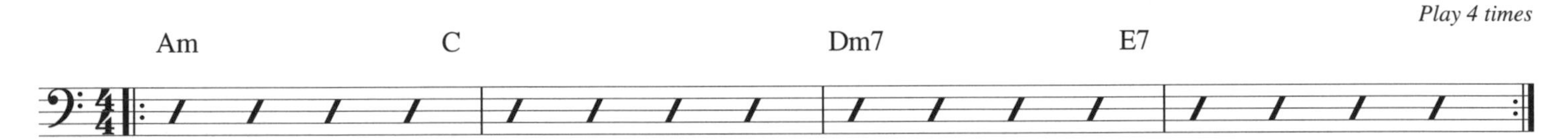

Slides

A great way to add spice to a bass line is to *slide* up or down the neck. To *slide*, strike a fretted note, then move that finger to the target note. There are two types of sliding: a grace-note slide (has no real rhythmic value) and a legato slide (has a specific time value). We'll try an example of both. There have been some great songs and lines built around a sliding part. Track 33 is for you to try out the sliding technique.

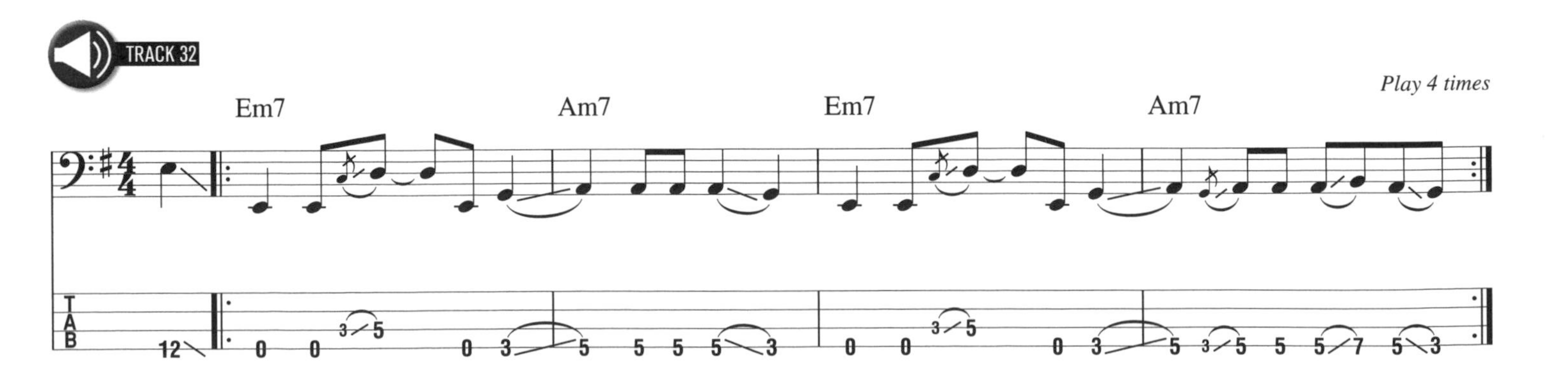

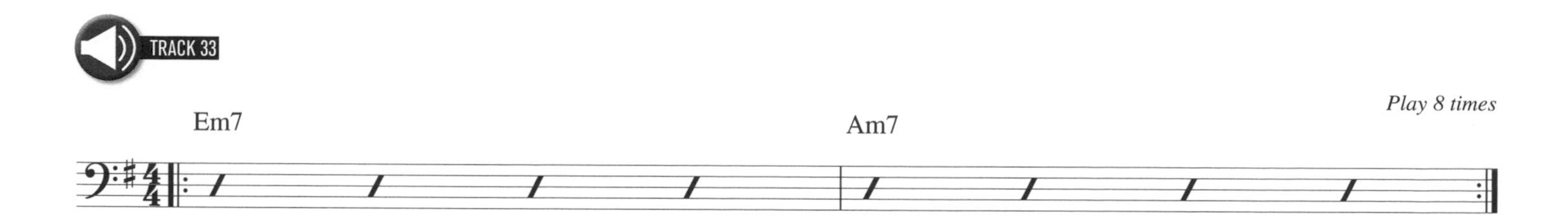

Vibrato

Another great technique that adds a little soul to your line is *vibrato. Vibrato* is widely used by guitar players and not as often by bassists. It can be purposely subtle or blatantly noticeable depending on what you are trying to project. It characteristically adds a singing quality to your bass line. *Bend vibrato* is created by pushing and pulling the string up and down with your fret hand after sounding a note. *Pivot vibrato* is achieved by pivoting your fretting finger back and forth. A *shake* is a rapid slide movement back and forth over a semitone.

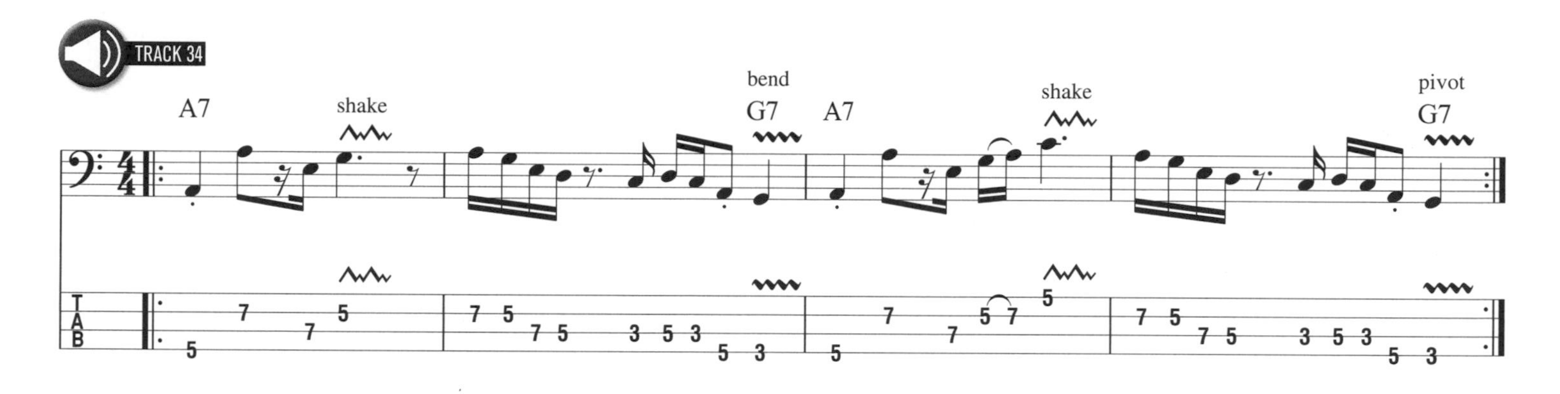

Slap & Pop

I'm assuming you know what slap and pop is, but we'll go over the technique briefly. If you want to delve deeper into this technique, there are some great resources out there. There are two parts to this technique: the thumb *slap* and the finger *pop*.

The *slap* is simply slapping the string against the fretboard with the side of your thumb. This is actually the trickiest part of the whole technique, so take your time to get it down right.

Let's start with your thumb: take your hand and ball it like a fist; then stick your thumb out. It should look like you're about to hitchhike, or you're giving someone a "thumbs up." With the side of your thumb, strike the string against the edge of the fingerboard. There are two ways to execute this movement and either is fine. We'll label them as the *bounce* and *follow through.*

The *bounce* is hitting the string directly in an up-down motion. The key to this movement is to quickly bounce off the string so it rings. With the *follow through*, you strike the string in a downward motion and follow through so that your thumb actually rests on the string below it. In both cases, strike the string hard enough so it gives off a percussive sound, not a plucking sound.

The most important part of this is to not move your thumb. This originates from your wrist/forearm, not your hand. To give you an idea of how this works, place your thumbs-up sign on a table, with your thumb in the air. Now, hit the table with your thumb by twisting your wrist/forearm.

The finger *pop* is pulling up the string so it snaps against the fingerboard to create a pop sound. You can use your index or middle finger, so find out what feels comfortable. As you improve, you may want to use both.

Let's go back to the thumbs-up sign. Loosen up your index or middle finger and create a hook with it. Placement for popping is directly above the fingerboard. After your thumb slaps, you can pop up in one movement. When finger popping, to get a nice snap sound from the string, place just enough of your finger under the string to grab it and pull up to get that sound. Popping too hard might break a string and popping too softly will sound like a pluck, not a pop. Listen for that in-between snap, which is not too hard and not too light. First we'll do some thumb exercises, then we'll combine popping. Each example is followed by a play-along track. A creative tip is to try slapping and popping an idea, then translate the same line into fingerstyle or vice versa to see what you come up with!

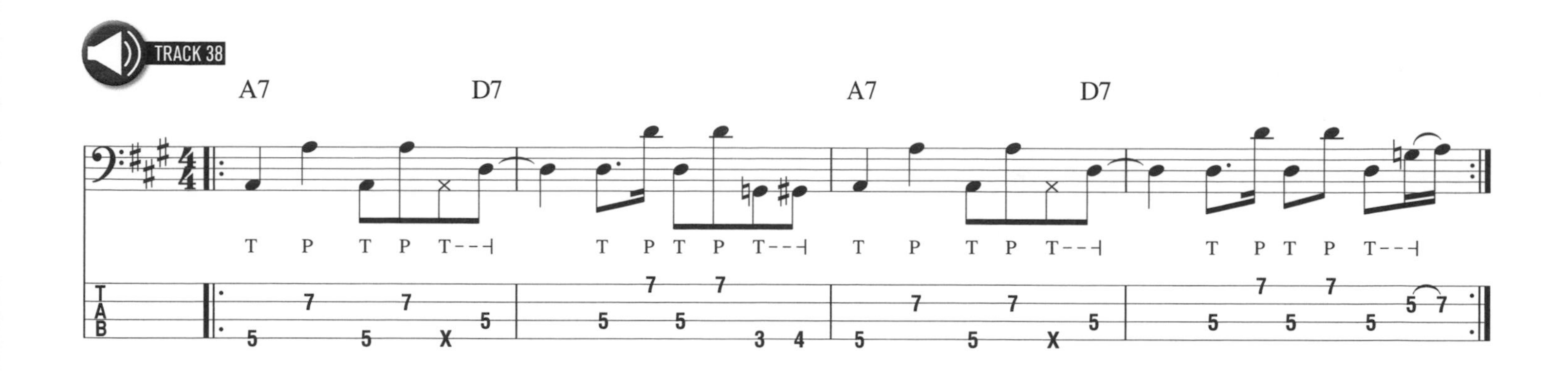

Moving On

OK, we could present a million examples incorporating slap, pop, fingerstyle, hammer-ons, slides, vibrato, using a pick, palm muting, dead notes, playing staccato or legato, but let's move on. If you are new to any of these techniques or concepts, be sure to spend some extra time on them. Create new bass parts, write new songs or riffs, and work it out so it becomes a natural part of your creative expression.

Other Techniques

In this chapter we've covered just a few of the possible techniques for the bass. They are tools for a toolbox, a method of creation. There are so many ways to create new sounds. People are still coming up with different ways to play the bass. Below are some other ways to come up with different sounds. Add some of your own ideas to the list.

- Tapping
- Harmonics
- Chords
- Alternate Tunings
- Different Plucking Techniques
- Different Slapping Techniques
- Different Fingering Techniques

Of course some techniques are not appropriate for some jobs, and sometimes being open to trying new things will inspire different ideas. If you are closed off to trying something, then that's one less way you will have to create. It's all up to you.

CHAPTER 5

Comfort Zone & Influences

Do you ever feel stuck or bored? In this chapter, we'll take a look at releasing and feeling inspired. We'll also look at our influences, the impact they have on our playing, and discovering our creative voice.

What Is Being Stuck?

Most musicians have experienced the phenomenon of being *stuck*. Sometimes it appears that no change is happening, regardless of how much effort is being put forth. This can create frustration, apathy, sadness, and various other negative feelings. It's not a fun place. It can be hard to be optimistic and open-minded when you feel like you are against a wall.

Being *stuck* is basically feeling creatively blocked. What does being in a creative zone feel like? How does the inverse feel? The difference is the feeling of loss and failure. If you haven't heard of the "fight or flight" response in psychology, it basically says that in certain situations humans will either confront or avoid their problems. When under pressure, people fight by working it out with determination, while others run (flight) as far away from the situation as possible.

The best way of becoming free to create is to have the awareness of what motivates you. What is your best creative environment? How can you succeed when you are uncomfortable or apathetic? Become unstuck by changing your thoughts and feelings. Everyone is different, so you must find out what will help you. Below are some suggestions. Please add to this list so the next time you are feeling this way you can regain your focus.

Ways to Re-Focus:

- Take a break and get into a better emotional state.
- Listen to or do something that inspires you.
- Be kind to yourself. The more limitations you impose on yourself, the harder it will be to focus.
- Ask for help. Have someone that you appreciate and admire give you creative input or advice.
- Ask yourself why you are frustrated and why you feel stuck. Having awareness of the "why" helps you get out of this mental attitude.
- Practice something that brings you joy and when you start feeling better, go back to what you did.
- Approach the idea from a different perspective. For example, if you are more technical, try singing a part. If you are not very theoretical, try the harmonic or rhythmic approaches. Just do something different than your usual way.

These are just some suggestions, so find what works best for you. It may be different every time, so be open and remember it is in your mind.

Responsibility & Taking Action

Another key to opening your creativity is taking on responsibility. What is responsibility? It is your "response ability." Get that? Your ability to respond. When working with others, no matter what the situation, all you can control is yourself and how you interact. You do have a choice. If you have a problem, you can either work it out or not. You can wait for the world and others to solve your problems (in which case you'll wait your entire life and feel horrible while you do) or, you can take action, move forward, and do something by your own volition. Being responsible is taking potential and power in your own hands.

Originality & Influences

Originality is thinking independently or inventing. This term is used in the music industry where, ironically, is anyone truly original? We've all grown up listening and being attracted to certain elements of music, styles, sounds, and so on. Even if you're a beginner, you have some kind of musical listening background which, in turn, has an impact or influence.

Speaking from a bass perspective, some of the most original players honor their influences. Are these players truly original or have they developed their own thing from a combination of influences? Some players try to emulate different instruments. Some take what other players only dabbled in to a whole new level by making it their own. What people often label as original, especially in music, is not really the definition of original. It's an evolution of a style, instrument, or technique. This is the way we'll use it here. We can put this to use by being open and embracing the ones that went before us.

I remember what Jaco Pastorius said, "Good musicians borrow and great musicians steal." What he meant was, embracing those who came before enables us to create and evolve by understanding what others have done. This can make us great musicians.

Aren't we, at some level, a mixture of influences? Not only music, but doesn't life itself influence us on a musical level? Look at how many songs and styles out there that are based on aggression or sadness. Basically, we are influenced by life itself and originality derives from influence and inspiration.

Visualize/Influence Exercise

Here is a great exercise to use when you get stuck or want to create, where you can borrow or steal from some of your influences. Keep in mind that you don't need to have the same mind or physical makeup to steal another person's style. It will always have "you" in it at some level. The goal here is for you to embrace your influences and come up with something all your own. I'll give you a few different styles of musical examples, and it's your job to visualize how your influences might play a bass part. Visualize yourself as the funkiest, heaviest, or most solid player. This exercise can help on a gig also. Say you are thinking too much about what's not working and the groove is suffering. A great way to get back in the music, and out of your head, is to visualize yourself as the way you'd like to be, then let go. Leonard Cohen once said, "Act the way you'd like to be and soon, you'll be the way you act."

For examples 40–44, the backing track will play without a bass part so you can come up with your own part. After a brief pause, the same track will be played again with a bass part for an example.

Visualize how someone you like might play these grooves and see what you can come up with.

Funk Example

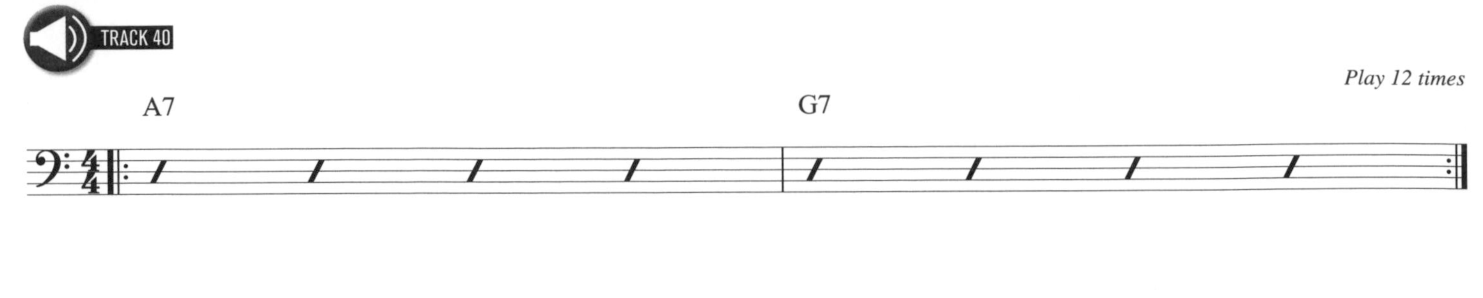

Rock Example

TRACK 41

Pop Example

TRACK 42

Progressive Metal Example

TRACK 43

Fusion Example

TRACK 44

What you'll start to notice is what you play comes out with your own interpretation, instead of sounding like some- one else.

Evolution

Evolution is the changes seen from one generation to the next. As bassists, how might this term help us be more creative and find our "original" voice? We've all seen the trend when a new player with a distinct approach comes to the forefront: legions of others attempt to copy his or her sound. We can say the same for bands and music as well. This isn't exactly a bad thing if you look at what these players have done. By just doing what they do, they inspire to help push forward a style of music, or a new way of playing or sounding. As a bassist, how can you evolve into a new original sound or style? If that is not what you want to do, how can you evolve in different ways just as a player or writer?

A good start in evolution is to define what you want. If you don't pay attention to what you want in life, you'll create by default. Creation becomes a reactive struggle versus proactive journey in achieving. Let's use an analogy: If you get in your car to drive and don't know where you want to go, you'll drive aimlessly wherever the road takes you. Sometimes that can be fun, but you'll always go somewhere without purpose. If you have an idea of the direction, let's say south, you'll get there sooner or later. But, if you have a clear and distinct idea, you can get out a map and commence the journey with confidence. What I'm getting at here is if you know what you want, you can have some concrete ways of getting there, and you can feel the anticipation of moving in that direction. That way you can enjoy the journey.

The Three C's

Comfort, **C**hange and **C**hoice are the *three C's.* Let me explain how they are applied:

1. Being *creative* is helpful when we feel comfortable enough to express ourselves. Sometimes we feel too comfortable and never push or allow ourselves to create. Be aware of whether you are feeling uncomfortable or too comfortable in this process. Are you evolving in the ways you want? Does a conscious change need to be made? Answer these questions for yourself.

2. *Change* is a constant in life. It is the one thing you can count on even though most of us try everything in our power to avoid it. Do you embrace change or fight it?

3. *Choice* is a touchy subject. Many don't believe they have a choice when, in fact, they do. We have a choice about everything in our path. Choices are made about everything. Take all the reasons/excuses away and a choice is being made everyday about how we live and create our life. Are you making choices or are you making excuses for choices not being made?

These three C's are for awareness and not for being hard on yourself. Stay positive and aware so you can make conscious choices about what you do and how you spend your time.

Moving Forward

This chapter was about forward movement and breaking free from your negative thoughts. You are only as limited as your thoughts and you are only as stuck as you feel. It is easier said than done, but if you keep at it you will find it easier to get unstuck all the time. You will find it easier to feel good and want to practice. You will embrace change and take responsibility. Embrace your influences; let them help you, not hamper you. Evolve.

CHAPTER 6

Groove

In this chapter, we'll look at the concept of *groove*. *Groove* means to furrow or cut. What that word means as a bassist, is to lay down a path that everyone and everything around the groove falls into. The way you approach the groove has a dramatic effect on the whole ensemble.

This is the word you've heard, or will hear more than any other word in your career! Many artists say that you can't teach someone how to groove and I tend to agree. Unfortunately, a lot of the time, bassists don't groove because they have not looked into why a line isn't grooving. We'll take a look at rhythm, space, pocket, and many other things that will help you interpret the groove.

Rhythm

Rhythm is the variation of the length and accentuation of a series of sounds or other events. In music, the medium we use to measure sound is written in notes. Even if you can't read music, I ask you to go through this section. It is loaded with helpful methods to interpret or change grooves by rhythmic placement. This section breaks down many common rhythms and brings to light some great ways to re-evaluate or interpret the groove.

Rhythmic Exploration

Most musicians tend to use the same rhythms in their approach to music, their tried and true method. When trying to come up with new grooves, drummers and bassists "feel" around until something hits or they modify the tried and true to make it fit. The next example breaks down rhythms so they are mathematical in approach, but very musically creative in application. It's a great way to work with a drummer to come up with kick drum and bass parts. This works if you find yourself having trouble coming up with new kick and bass patterns, or if you want to break out of the box and try new things. If you can't read these rhythms, just get the rhythms in your head so you can use them.

The audio tracks have the drummer and bassist locking into different rhythmic patterns. These patterns only scratch the surface of the possibilities one can come up with. All examples have the kick-drum pattern written out so you can see the relation between kick drum and bass.

This example will have the kick drum playing quarter notes on beats 1 and 3. The bass will explore different ways to play around this seemingly simple pattern. Keep in mind that all the drummer has to do for variety is change up his cymbal or snare pattern. On the repeat, the bass drops out so you can play.

I could have written out several more pages of different rhythms (just think if I added notes other than G). Do you see all the possible ideas just using rhythm?

This next example will change the kick drum and bass rhythms every two measures. As before, the bassist can interpret that in many different ways, but we will stick just to the kick-drum pattern. Try it yourself on the repeat.

This is again just a small amount of kick and bass patterns.

The next two examples are for you to try some ideas along with the kick drum. Try locking in with the kick, then try different pitches from the chord. Try anything and see how it sounds.

Previously, all we did was keep a consistent kick drum on beats 1 and 3. Drummers will often change things up, which opens all kinds of options.

Tips for Rhythm Exploration:

- Pick a rhythm figure and write ideas and bass lines with it.
- When playing with a drummer, decide what rhythm you'll lock in with when creating a new idea.
- Listen to the snare and try playing with that too, or rest and leave space when the snare hits.
- Remember staccato and legato approaches when trying different rhythms.
- Play on and off with the kick.
- Add in the other concepts from this chapter.

Busy or Spacious

Another way to explore rhythm is to either play busy (with a lot of rhythm) or to play spacious (using less notes). More notes can tend to drive a song and add energy, while less notes can create a more solid foundation and coherence. How you approach this idea is up to you. The key to making the choice is by listening. Listen to what the rest of the band is playing and decide what the song needs. If you are coming up with a part for the band to play to, see how it sounds with the band as you listen to what's going on.

Let's try an example with a spacious part, then switch to a busier part using the same example.

Now try it for yourself. Create a bass line that's busy, spacious, or a combination of both. Come up with several different parts.

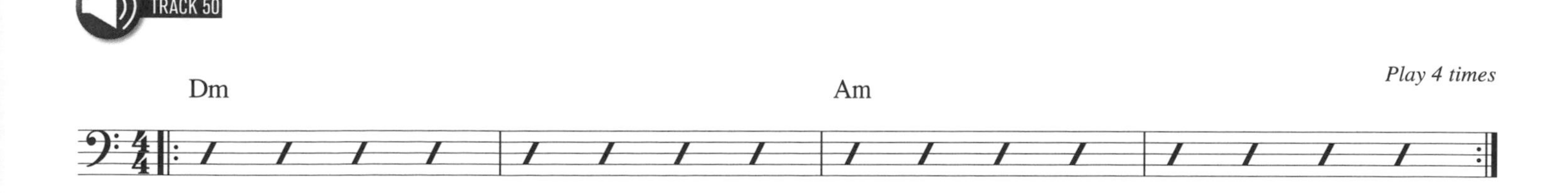

Melodic or Rhythmic

Melodic playing is infusing melodic ideas into a part, like playing a melody. It is a great way to really make a part stand out or carry a song in a different fashion. Using different notes from the chord structure is the usual method, or just use your ears to come up with melodic phrases (Paul McCartney, from the Beatles, was a master at this). On the other end, playing rhythmically is being spacious or busy, locking in with the kick, and using root notes to anchor the chord movement. We are using the same backing track from tracks 49 and 50 to show you that there are many possibilities for bass lines over the same chords and drum beat. First, we'll play a melodic idea, then a rhythmic one. Go back to track 50 after this example and try it yourself.

Here are some examples for you to try a melodic or rhythmic approach.

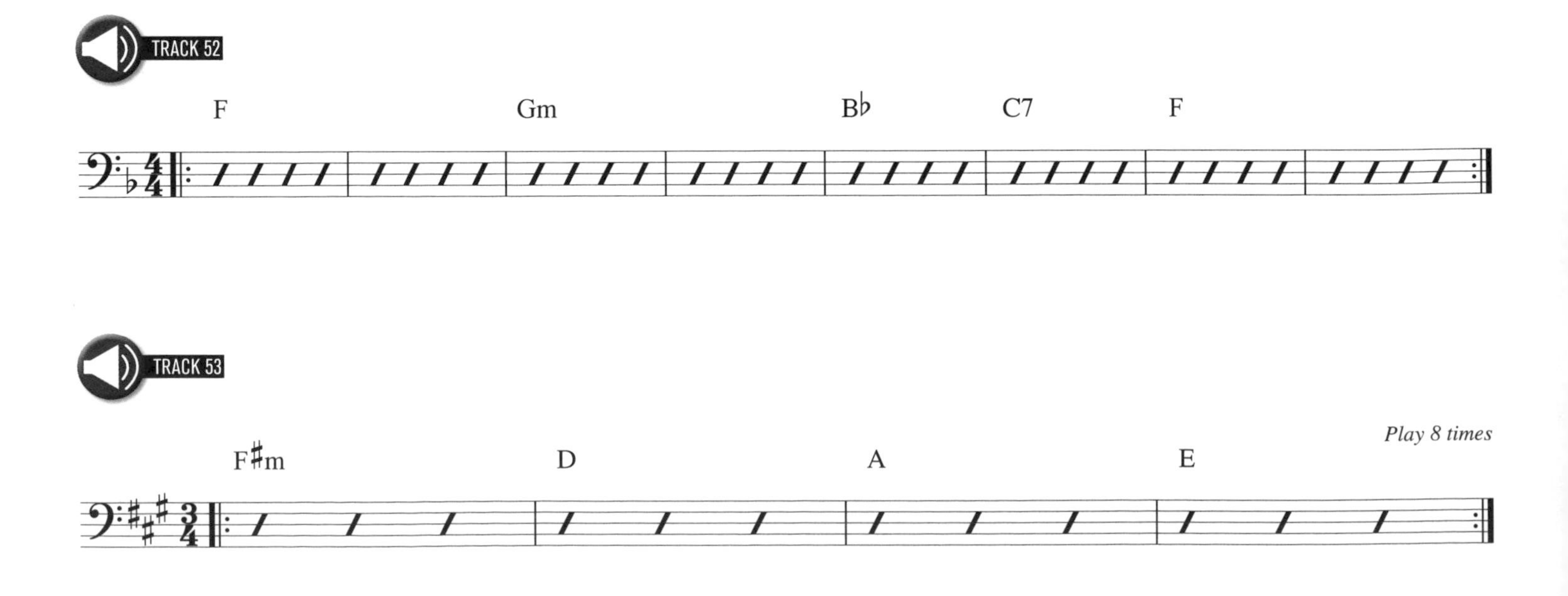

As you can see, there are many approaches to inspire ideas. If you get frustrated with one approach, try another and see what comes out.

The Pocket

Another term used in music, especially in relation to bass and drums, is called the *pocket*. Remember the definition of groove? The *pocket* is essentially the same thing but, to add a little twist, you have some room to move. The concept is called *pushing* or *pulling* the pocket. You can actually push and pull without speeding up or slowing down. You have three ways to play the pocket, you can *push*, play *right on*, or *pull*. This is an art and takes great time feel to accomplish; some players do it without even knowing. The first step is awareness. Can you drag without slowing down or push without speeding up? We'll take a look at this concept; it is extremely subtle and extremely effective.

Right On

Playing *right on* the pocket is playing exactly with the click, which is a great starting place for any groove. Being human, we tend to fluctuate within the groove, so playing right on is like being a human metronome.

Push

Pushing, or playing on top of the groove, gives a driving impression to the feel. If a groove is lacking drive or attitude, try pushing the feel to add that extra aggression to a bass line.

Pull

Pulling, or playing behind the beat, gives a laid back and smooth feel. It is really prominent in R&B to lay back and let the pocket breathe. This is known as a *deep pocket*.

Many players are unaware of their own pocket, which is why certain types of players just can't find the groove when playing unfamiliar music that requires a different approach to the pocket. When playing with drummers, having a good time feel can work to your advantage or demise. The rhythm section lays the foundation and if a drummer pulls while you push the pocket, it can leave the rest of the band wondering what's going on, or why it doesn't feel good. Playing with a drummer is about listening and flowing with how each other is playing the pocket. Sometimes it can be magical and sometimes it needs to be discussed if it isn't happening. All players move in the pocket, so the ability to move with the direction and take charge makes all the difference in the world. When working with a drum machine, the groove can be up to you because the tempo does not fluctuate. If you want a more laid-back vibe, pull your bass line a little and see how that feels. It's all about awareness!

Where Do You Play?

With all the new recording technologies, not only can you hear the subtle differences of pushing and pulling, you can also see visually what's going on.

If you can't quite hear it at this point, perhaps seeing it when recording might be helpful. Below are pictures of three audio waveforms showing the bass line and click track. Can you see the difference? Now listen to track 54. A drum part will also be playing along so you can hear the relation to the kick and bass. The kick will be right on the beat, while the bass part is played right on, pushed, and pulled (in that order).

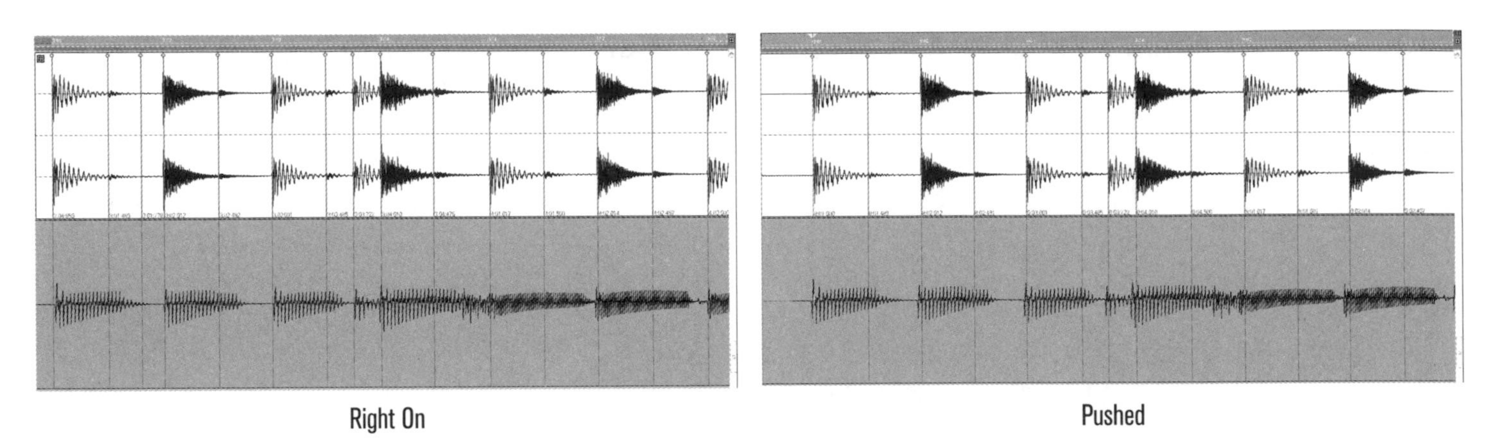

Right On

Pushed

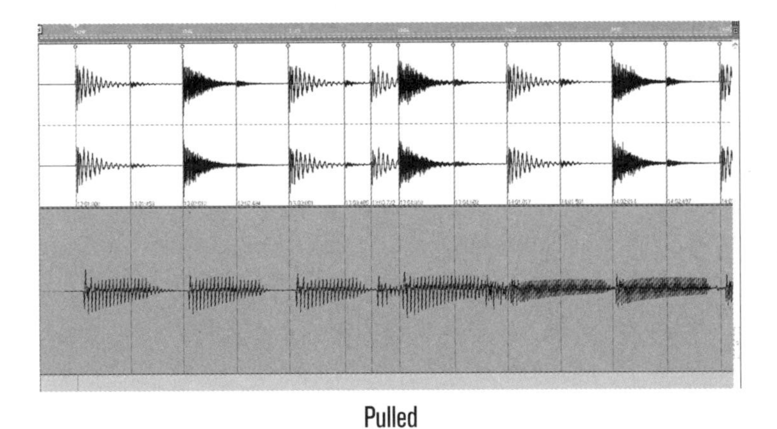

Pulled

Shuffle Feel

When grooving, a rhythmic feel called a *triplet*, *swing*, or *shuffle feel* can really enhance a bass line and bring it to life. In a *shuffle feel*, eighth notes are played unevenly and transferred to a triplet feel. Three eighth notes become a triplet where the first eighth note is the value of two, so it is essentially twice as long as the second note. This gives the groove a bouncy feel.

Triplet or shuffle notation would be hard to read , so you'll often see straight-eighth notes with the word "swing" or ♫ = ♩♪ written at the beginning of a song. Here is an example of adding a triplet feel to an eighth-note groove. We'll play it straight the first time, then add the shuffle feel.

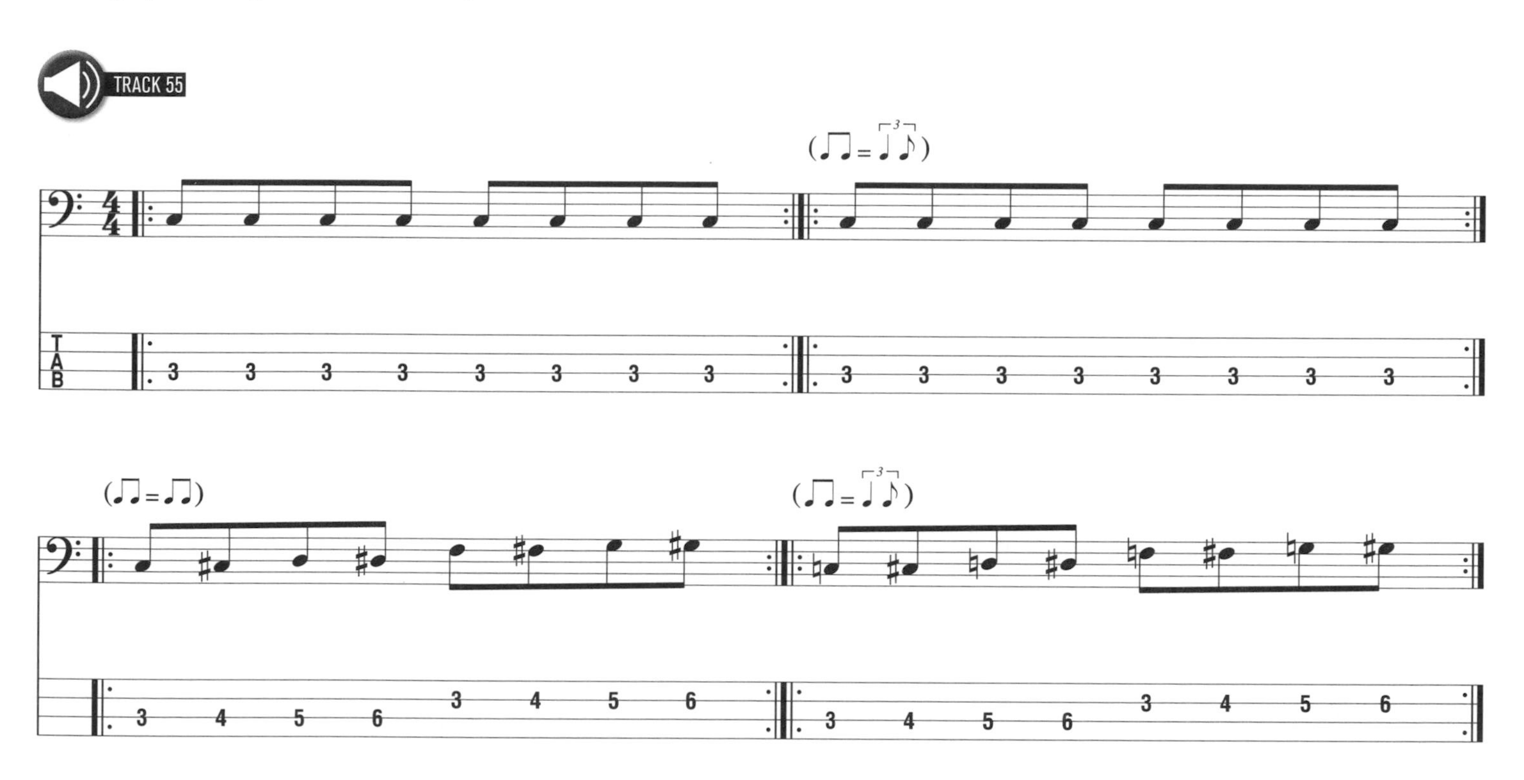

As you can hear, this creates another way to try something different. Add a slight shuffle feel to your groove and see what you come up with.

Dynamics

Dynamics are the ability to play loud and soft. In a song, playing louder during the chorus and softer during the verse is standard protocol. Dynamics is an overall concept of building the big picture. Within that big picture, which we'll call the bass line, how and where we place dynamics on each note will affect the groove. The ability to technically execute notes with dynamic control is an art in itself. To show you how effective dynamics can be, listen to track 56. The first time, it will be played all at one dynamic level, and the second time it will be executed by *accenting* (playing louder) beats 2 and 4. This is notated with an accent mark ♩.

Technically, playing hard is easier than playing soft. Having control and executing notes quietly is the key to a clean, vibrant sound. If you are playing hard and want to accent a note, you have to play even harder. Oftentimes, harder comes out sounding sloppy and uncontrolled. Try tracks 57 and 59 and see how this works for you.

Dynamic Groove

Now that we've looked at the execution of dynamics, we'll put it to use. In most cases, especially in jazz and blues, accenting on beats 2 and 4 makes the groove happen in a big way. The same goes for funk songs, and in songs with harmonically dense bass lines. A well-placed accent goes a long way in a groove. If you are playing a bass line and it is not grooving, try placing an accent. This awareness develops with experience and experimentation. Play along with track 59 and have at it.

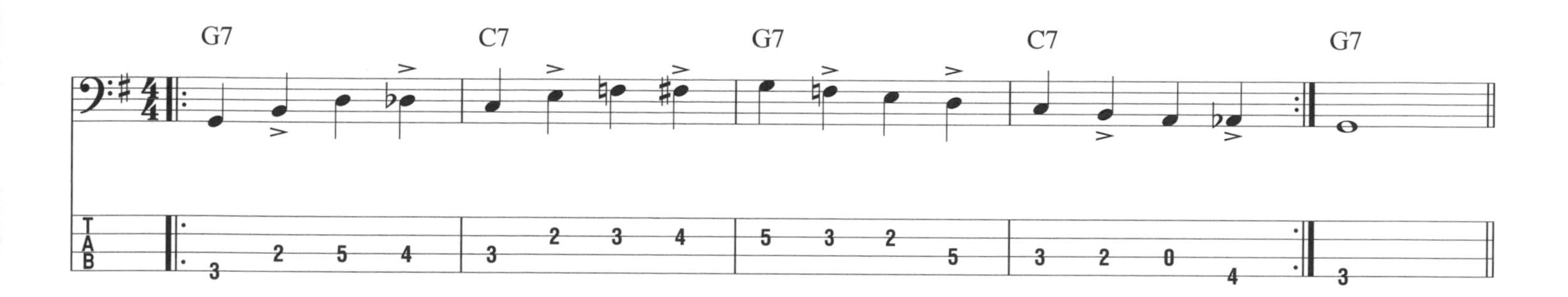

This is a brief overview of a much broader subject, so try it on your own. Listen and see how accenting in different places within a measure creates a different feel. It's like talking; if everyone spoke at the same volume they would sound monotone and like a robot. Consider the same with your bass parts; let them be like expressive speaking, sometimes soft, sometimes loud, and with different inflections.

Creative Groove Checklist

When establishing a groove, the first thing to do is listen. Play simple and get the feel. Determine the pocket and go through a checklist if you feel as though your part could be better:

- Does it groove?
- How would it sound if it was busier or more spacious?
- Should it be treated with a rhythmic or melodic approach?
- Would adding accents on certain beats enhance the groove?
- Should you lay back, push, or play straight?
- Should you employ a shuffle feel to the line?
- What might an influence (bassist/musician) do?
- Visualize.
- Try different techniques.
- Try an effect.
- Approach using the different areas of music (Chapter 2).

The funny thing is that most times when we are stuck, it's because we didn't look at all the options available!

CHAPTER 7

Harmony

Harmony, or theory, is basically the knowledge of music. The "why" that helps us discover the "how to" and the language that helps musicians communicate. In this chapter, we will go through chords, scales, and note choice to help discover the available options in music's creation. We'll review basic harmony and assume that you're familiar with some theory. If you aren't, I can't stress enough how much easier playing and creativity will be with theoretical knowledge. Take theory lessons or purchase method books that cover harmony in a more detailed fashion for you to truly understand these topics.

Why Theory?

Theory is the language of music. The goal is to express ourselves creatively. If we are limited in our communication, how can we express ourselves to our fullest potential? Having knowledge is like having the key to a locked door you can open anytime and in any situation.

Theory isn't expression, it is a tool. There is a world of great players who don't know a lot about theory or haven't had lessons, but can express themselves just fine. Having no formal training does not imply theoretical obliviousness. Being aware and knowledgeable does not hinder, it can only help. It is what one does with the knowledge that helps create.

The Power of Note Choice

Having the knowledge of chords is like having a schematic to a device that you are working with. If you know how it works, then you can take it apart, put it back together, modify it, add to it, and build one of your own. Being armed with chord knowledge as a bassist can change the way a whole song or idea is heard. The root note of a chord is not your only choice.

The next track is a preliminary example for you to hear what different choices can happen over a simple triad (a three-note chord). The background will be playing a G triad, the notes of which are G, B, and D. The bass will play a G for four measures, change to playing chord tones, then notes from the G major scale. On the CD, the whole example repeats again so you can try your own ideas.

This is an extremely simple example that shows how much you can move a song into new territory.

Bass is the connection between the rhythm and harmony of any band, controlling the feel and harmony while gluing it all together. We'll expand on chords, but first let's go through the scale from which chords are built and the keys from which scales derive.

Key Signatures

Key signatures are the backbone to the structure of harmony/theory. Key signatures tell you the appropriate seven notes for the musical situation. If you understand key signatures more deeply, they also tell you the chords and scales built from those seven notes.

This grid goes through the major keys and their corresponding minor key. Now you know what notes to play when someone says, "this song is in the key of _____________."

KEY	NUMBER OF SHARPS OR FLATS	NOTES IN KEY/SCALE
C major/ A minor	No Sharps or Flats	C, D, E, F, G, A, B
G major/ E minor	One Sharp	G, A, B, C, D, E, F♯
D major/ B minor	Two Sharps	D, E, F♯, G, A, B, C♯
A major/ F♯ minor	Three Sharps	A, B, C♯, D, E, F♯, G♯
E major/ C♯ minor	Four Sharps	E, F♯, G♯, A, B, C♯, D♯
B major/ G♯ minor	Five Sharps	B, C♯, D♯, E, F♯, G♯, A♯
F♯ major/ D♯ minor	Six Sharps	F♯, G♯, A♯, B, C♯, D♯, E♯
C♯ major/ A♯ minor	Seven Sharps	C♯, D♯, E♯, F♯, G♯, A♯, B♯
F major/ D minor	One Flat	F, G, A, B♭, C, D, E
B♭ major/ G minor	Two Flats	B♭, C, D, E♭, F, G, A
E♭ major/ C minor	Three Flats	E♭, F, G, A♭, B♭, C, D
A♭ major/ F minor	Four Flats	A♭, B♭, C, D♭, E♭, F, G
D♭ major/ B♭ minor	Five Flats	D♭, E♭, F, G♭, A♭, B♭, C
G♭ major/ E♭ minor	Six Flats	G♭, A♭, B♭, C♭, D♭, E♭, F
C♭ major/ A♭ minor	Seven Flats	C♭, D♭, E♭, F♭, G♭, A♭, B♭

Intervals

An *interval* is defined as the distance in pitch between two notes.

A *half step* is the smallest interval in Western music. A half step is measured on the bass by one fret.

A *whole step* is equal to two half steps, or two fret spaces.

When relating to scales, intervals are named after the number of notes they span from the root of the scale. For example, in a C major scale the notes are C–D–E–F–G–A–B. The second note of the scale is D, therefore called a 2nd. The third note is E and is called a 3rd. G is the fifth note which is the 5th. Playing a one octave scale, we have the root, 2nd, 3th, 4th, 5th, 6th, 7th, and the octave.

When an interval exceeds an octave, it is called a *compound interval.* Some intervals, especially on bass, don't sound appealing played together in the first octave because of the low frequencies, or the pitches are too close. This is when compound intervals are used. Compound intervals (known as chord extensions) continue with the theme of counting after an octave. An octave is an 8th, so the 9th is the same as a 2nd. An octave above the 3rd is a 10th, and so on.

The thing to remember is that intervals sound different and are considered major, minor, or perfect depending on the amount of whole and half steps they have in between them.

Major/Minor/Perfect

Scales are built from intervals, and it is the distance between those intervals that creates a specific type of sound which is major or minor. Perfect means it is the same intervallic distance both in major and minor.

Here is the relation of intervals in distance from the root (or *tonic*) (remember a half step = one fret and a whole step = two frets):

- Major Second = 1 Step
- Minor Third = 1 1/2 Step
- Major Third = 2 Steps
- Perfect Fourth = 2 1/2 Steps
- Sharp Fourth or Flat Fifth = 3 Steps
- Perfect Fifth = 3 1/2 Steps
- Minor Sixth = 4 Steps
- Major Sixth = 41/2 Steps
- Minor Seventh = 5 Steps
- Major Seventh = 5 1/2 Steps

Scales

Scales are, basically, seven notes built from a series of whole and half steps. Major and minor sounds are based on whole steps and half steps. The way whole and half steps are arranged determines sounds that create different types of scales and chords. The reason scales on fretted instruments can be memorized by shape is because of the geometric relationship of whole and half steps.

Let's break down the major and minor scale by intervals. Keep in mind there are more than one major and minor scale, but these two are considered the standard.

- *Major scale intervals:* Whole, Whole, Half, Whole, Whole, Whole, Half
- *Minor scale intervals:* Whole, Half, Whole, Whole, Half, Whole, Whole

As stated before, the bass fretboard is geometric and scale shapes are congruent throughout in standard tuning. Here are some scale shapes you can move all over to play in different keys. The tonic (starting note) names the scale.

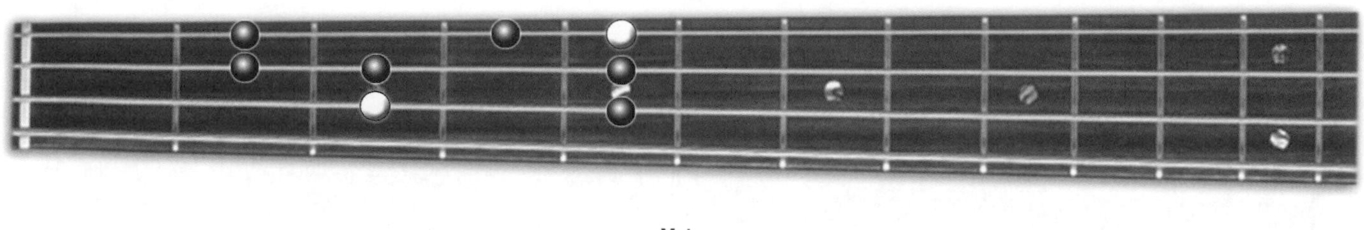

Major

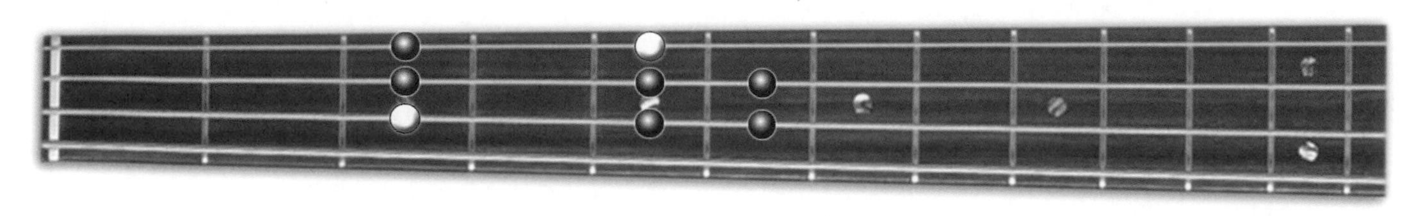

Minor

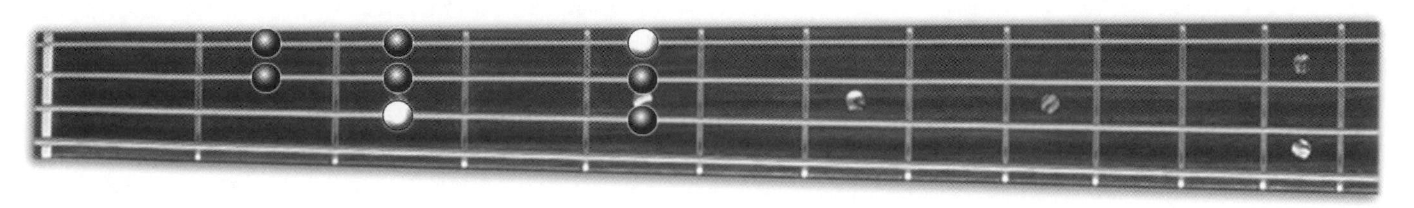

Dominant

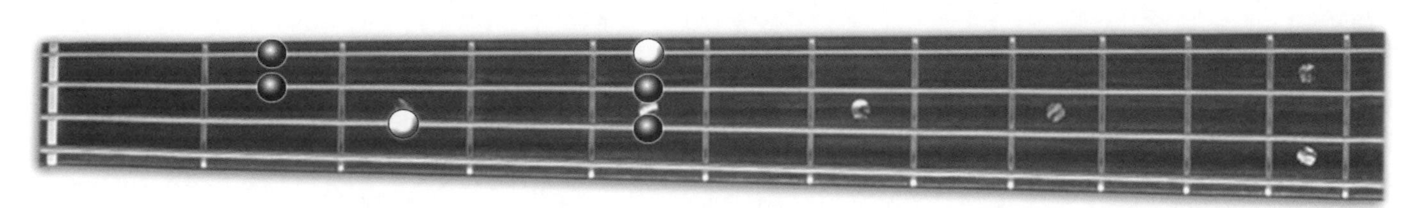

Major Pentatonic

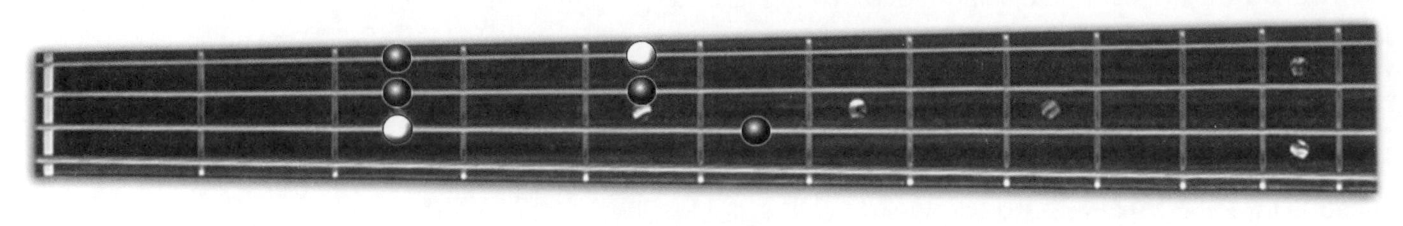

Minor Pentatonic

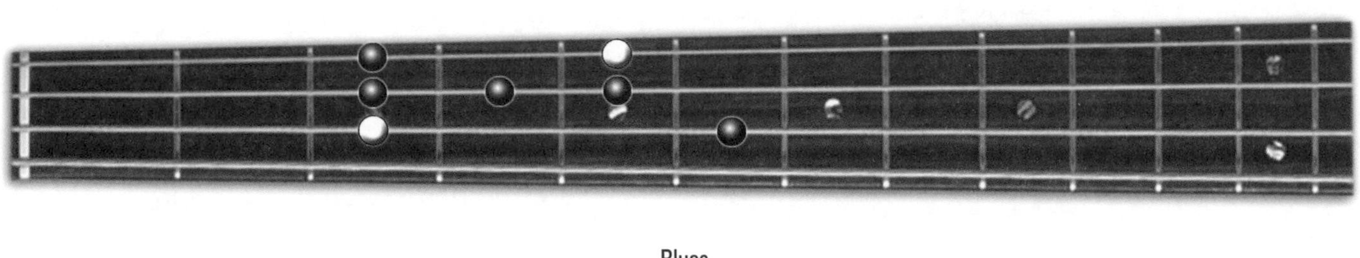

Blues

Let's create some parts using three of the scales mentioned. These enable you to come up with melodic lines, parts, fills, or even riffs. For the next three examples, the backing track follows so you can create your own part.

Major Scale

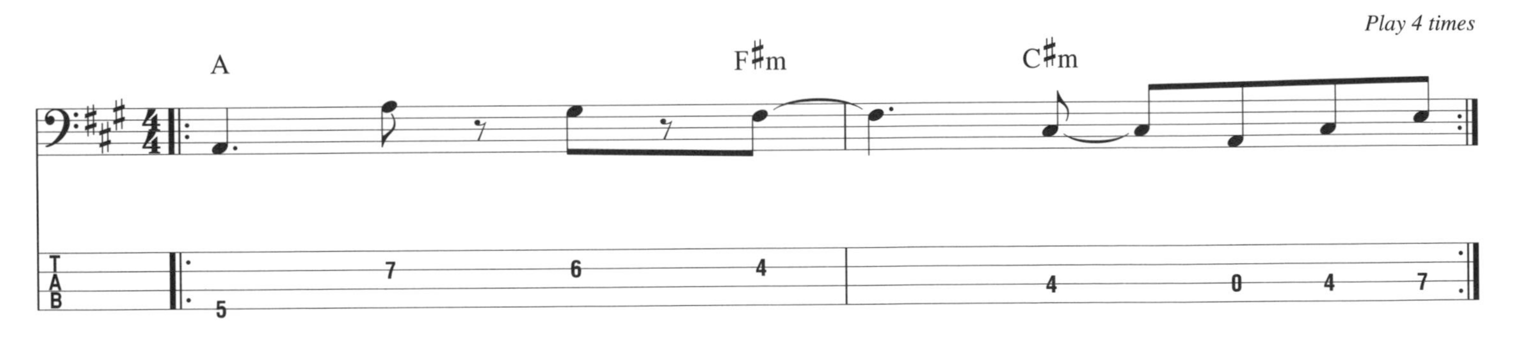

Your turn!

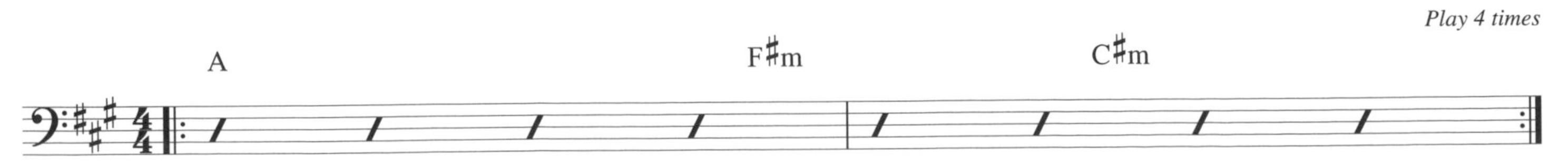

Minor Scale

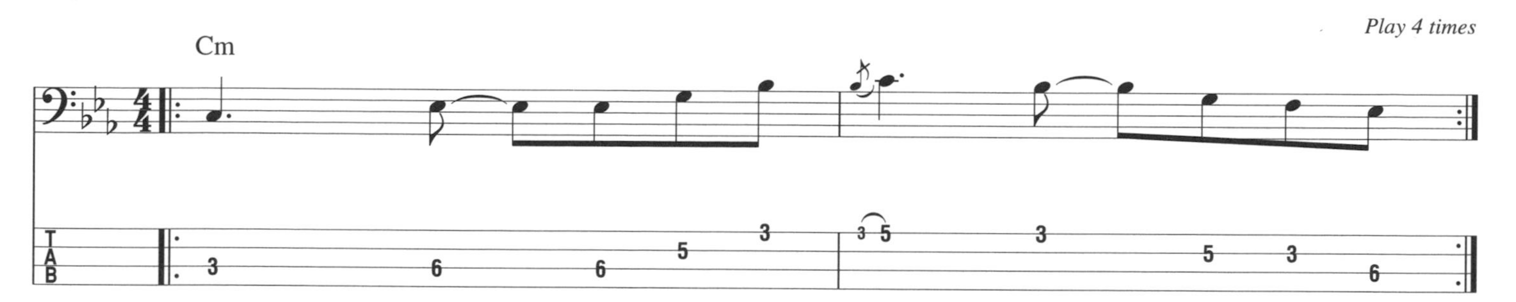

Play 4 times

Cm

Dominant Scale

Play 4 times

D7

Modes

The *modes* are the seven scales built from each note in a specific key. When you pick a key, there are seven diatonic scales that correspond to each note in that key. If you memorize these scales and their qualities, playing in "key" will be a breeze.

In the key of C, the notes are C–D–E–F–G–A–B. If you play all these notes in that order, you have a C major scale. If you start on a different note, let's say D, and play the same notes starting from D, you are still playing notes from the key of C. Because of the half step and whole step changes starting on D, it takes the shape and sound of a different scale.

Each note of every key has a corresponding scale and chord. So, in every key we have seven scales and seven chords. The great thing is that all you have to do is memorize these seven scales and apply them, because they are the same shapes for each key.

This section is a brief overview of the modes in C.

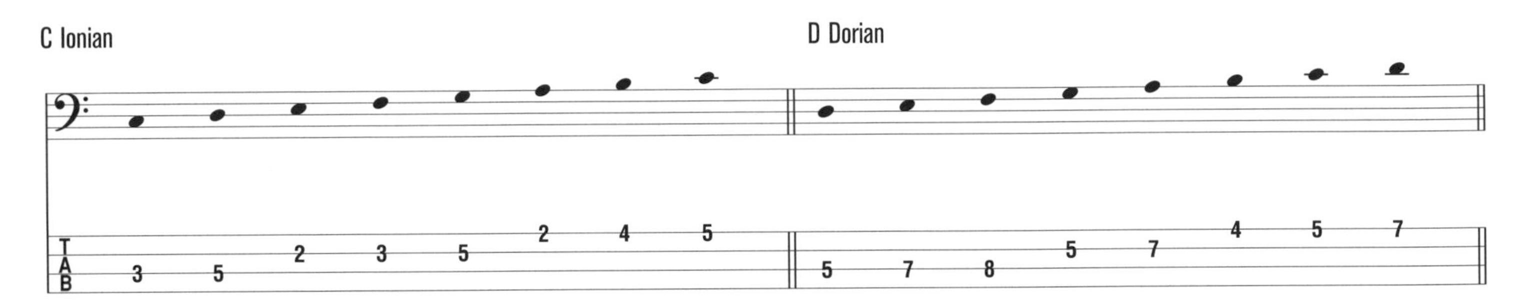

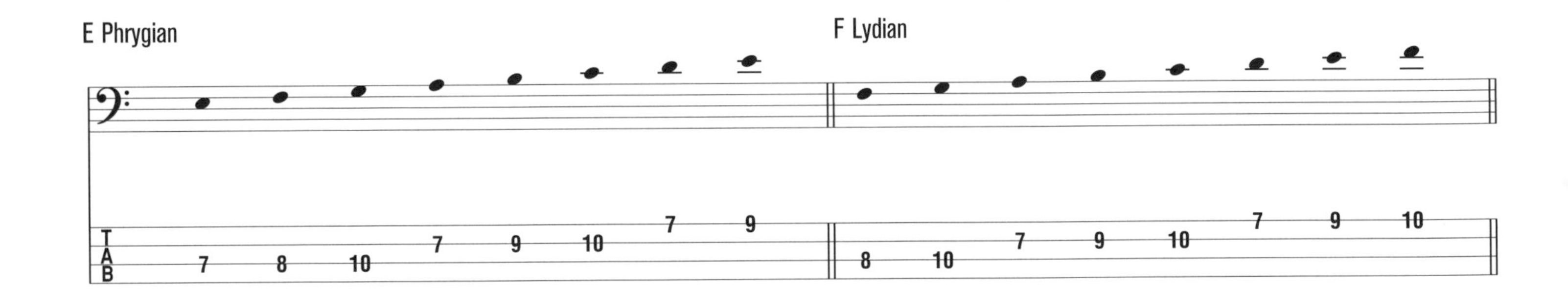

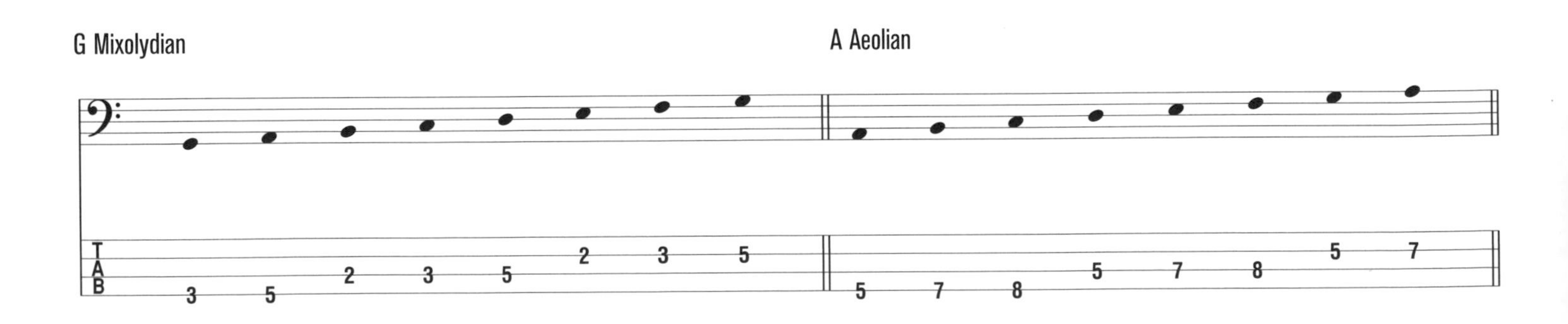

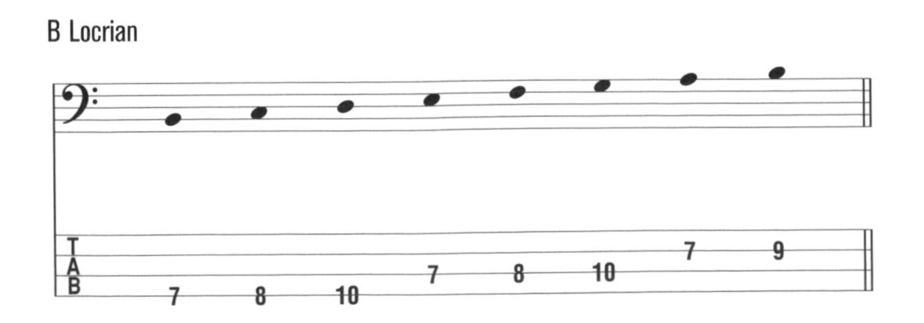

Just like the movable scales in the previous section, these modes are movable. If you are in the key of G, the Ionian scale starts on G, A Dorian, B Phrygian, C Lydian, D Mixolydian, E Aeolian, and F♯ Locrian. (If this is the first time you've heard of modes, don't worry. There is endless information available on the modes.)

Each one of these scales has its own sound and can create different vibes and melodies. If you were approaching the modes from a chord standpoint in the key of C, you'd have C major, D minor, E minor, F major, G major, A minor, and B half diminished.

For the next examples, the chord progressions are based on diatonic modal harmony. I'll write what modes are being implied by the chord progression, so you come up with the bass part.

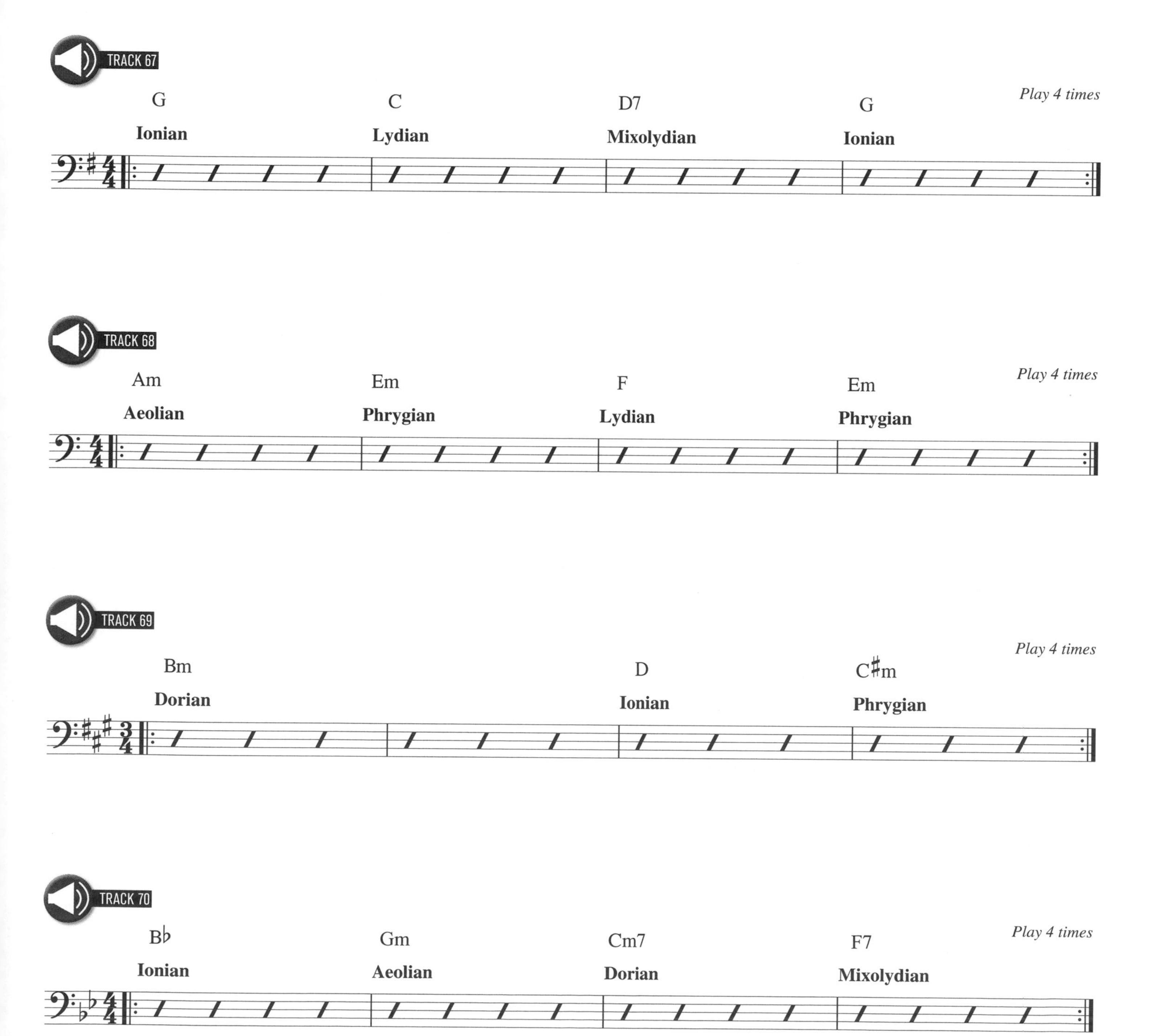

Using Scales

There are many scales out there with unique sounds. Creating parts using a slightly different scale can make a riff or a melody. Use your ears and open yourself to all the options. Just knowing whether a chord is major or minor can give you unlimited potential.

Search for lessons on modes or exotic scales to expand your scale knowledge and learn to hear the different scales so they become a natural form of expression. Musicians are using them all the time and don't even know it. Build melodic ideas or melodies, write riffs around a particular scale, and create grooves that have weird intervals. Come up with whatever you can and have fun with the scales and harmony. It all depends on how you look at it.

It is important to understand the relationship these modes have to the chords being played. If you know the chords and what actual notes are in the chord, you can color the sound by your scale choice.

Chords

Chords are the building blocks of music. They create a structure for harmony and melody. As a bassist, knowing chords is essential to exploring and creating. If you have great ears you can get by, but having great ears AND chord knowledge will make you unstoppable. Following is a list of chord structures and how they are built from an intervallic standpoint.

Triads

Triads are three-note voicings. They can be major, minor, or diminished. We will elaborate on diminished and half-diminished later. A triad consists of the root, third, and fifth of a scale played together as a chord.

Major triad is the root, major third, and perfect fifth.
Minor triad is the root, minor third, and perfect fifth.
Diminished triad is the root, minor third, and flat fifth.

Chord Types

Let's break down chord symbols so you understand what they mean. We will use C as the root in all these examples where R = Root and m = Minor.

Major

A major chord, in its simplest form, is a triad. If you add other intervals, it is labeled with those intervals including the triad in the chord structure. Remember 9th = 2nd, 11th = 4th, 13th = 6th.

- C is a triad
- Cmaj6 is a triad with a 6th added
- Cmaj7 is a triad with a 7th added

Note: The standard rule is that chords are built from top to bottom in 3rds as in R, 3, 5, 7, 9, 11, 13.

- Cmaj9 is a triad, 7th, and 9th
- Cmaj11 is a triad, 7th, 9th, and 11th
- Cmaj13 is a triad, 7th, 9th, and 13th

When using extensions like 9th, 11th, and 13th, sometimes it is physically impossible to include all the notes implied by the chord symbol. This is why chord players will pick and choose which notes to address.

Sharp and Flat

You'll also see extensions *flatted* (♭) or *sharped* (♯). This means you lower, or raise (respectively), the interval by a half step.

add

You'll sometimes see the word *add* in a chord symbol. This means you add the note on top of the existing label instead of the building from 3rds rule. For example, a Cadd9 chord has a triad and a 9th without addressing the 7th.

sus

Sus means to suspend the 3rd. A sus4 chord is built with the R, 4th, and 5th and a sus2 chord means R, 2nd, and 5th. Sus always suspends the 3rd and the interval labeled takes its place.

Minor

A *minor chord* is a minor triad. The same rules for major chords apply to minor chords except that you are building from the minor scale in 3rds.

- Cm is a minor triad
- Cm6 = minor triad with an added 6th
- Cm7 = minor triad with the 7th added
- Cm9 is the R, 3, 5, 7, 9 of the minor scale
- Cm11 is the R, 3, 5, 7, 9, 11 of the minor scale
- Cm(maj)7 = minor triad with a major 7th

Dominant

Dominant chords are huge in blues and jazz. It is a major triad with a minor 7th. It creates tension because of its sound. Whenever you see a chord letter with a 7, it means dominant.

- C7 = major triad and a flat 7th
- C9 = major triad and flat 7th and a 9th
- C7sus4 = R, 4th, 5th, flat 7th

Diminished and Half Diminished

A *diminished* chord is a stack of minor 3rds.

- C°= R, minor 3rd, flat 5th
- C°7 = R, minor 3rd, flat 5th, and double flatted 7th

Half diminished can be seen two ways: as a minor7♭5 or half diminished.

- Cø7, Cm7♭5 = R, minor 3rd, flat 5th, minor 7th

Augmented

Augmented is a major chord with a sharp 5th.

- C+ = R, 3rd, sharp 5th
- C+7 = R, 3rd, sharp 5th, minor 7th

Power Chords

Power chords are just the root and the 5th, so they don't technically have a major/minor quality.

Slash Chords

These are chords with a specific note in the bass other than the root (yes, this means you). Often seen as a chord with an alternate bass note on the other side of a slash.

- C/G = C triad with G in the bass
- Cm/E♭ = C minor triad with E♭ in the bass
- C7/G = C dominant chord with G in the bass

Some confusion can arise with slash chords due to a music chart and its intended reader. Some guitar charts use this method to help the guitarist find the right fingering for a chord and you, as a bassist, would not play that slash. Most often it is intended for bass or piano; just be aware that if it does not sound good, try the root instead.

More on Chords and Scales

As you can see, most chords are built on 3rds unless indicated. Armed with this knowledge, you can imply several different scales over a minor chord as long as the scale has a minor 3rd in it. It's the same for major; if the scale has a major 3rd and no 7th, you can use Lydian, Ionian, or Mixolydian depending on what sound you are creating. The notes in between the chord tones are what make the line interesting. All you have to do is have the ears to hear it and the knowledge to apply it.

For decades musicians have pushed the envelope by playing over progressions using different scales, harmonies, ideas, and concepts. All you have to do is look and study and you'll find a wealth of knowledge about playing over chords and scales.

Now let's work through some grooves with different chords. I will play a bass part for each example first.

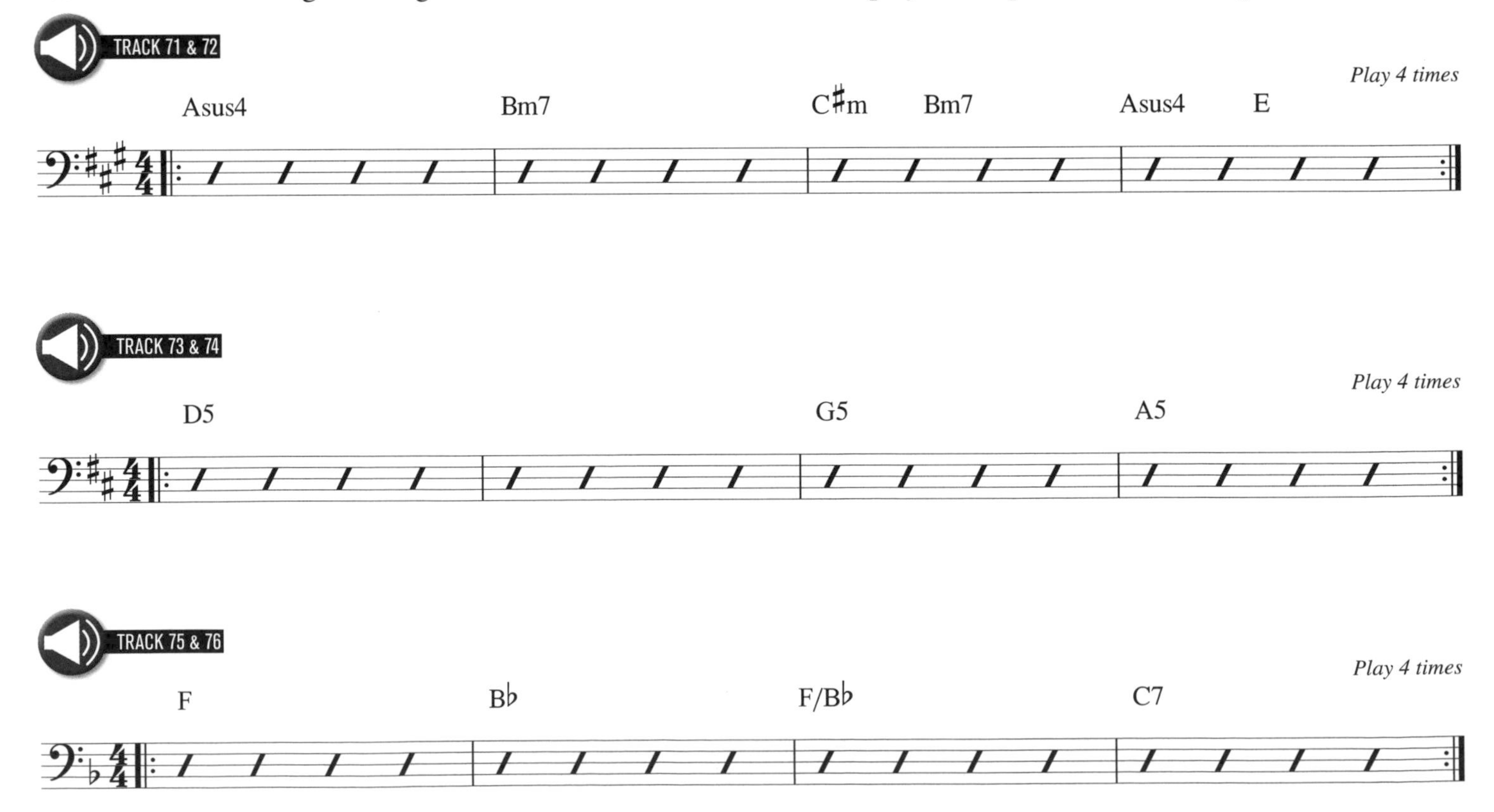

CHAPTER 8

Styles & Listening

On the road to opening up your creativity, being informed about different styles and listening to different forms of music can broaden your approach. If you go back in history, you'll see how music has formed, moved from one style to another, and how the merging of styles made new forms of music. It's hard to find a band that you can label as simple rock anymore. There is pop rock, grunge rock, '80s rock, progressive rock, classic rock, and metal. I could go on for days with all the genres and sub-genres for rock alone, not to mention all the other styles of music. Let's take a deeper look at ways to expand the creative senses by infusing different styles.

Breaking What Rules?

How has new music arrived and changed from different styles? How have players developed techniques and approaches that have taken music and instruments to new levels? Frankly, those who did this broke the unwritten rules of the ideas others had. Sometimes these bands and individuals had to break though the ridicule, judgment, and slow success to finally achieve a new or fresh thing. The people who paved the way often did so without support. They had a vision and drive to succeed while playing what they wanted. You see this in anything where people have paved a trail. There was a way everyone followed, unquestioningly, until someone came along, broke the rules, and made a new way. These days it isn't as hard because we are at a new open era of creative influence. However, many do stay within the boundaries of unspoken rules of how things "should" be. Go back to the beginning of this book and really dig deep if you have not done so, and find your vision of what you want creatively. It can really help you to define what it is you want.

Infusing Different Styles

An entire book could be written on the topic of combining styles alone. This will be a brief overview to spark some ideas of ways to open the creative pathways. You can blend styles by stealing (remember the Jaco quote?) or borrowing ideas that work in one style, and bring it to another. The key to doing this is to listen and learn. Study different types of music with an open mind and find the elements you like and learn them. Let's come up with a list of ways to blend styles and put a few of them to use:

- Write down various groove styles and try them over an already written idea.
- Come up with a riff based off of an exotic scale or a different genre of music.
- Buy a book on different rhythms and try to incorporate them.
- Use a drum or piano book to come up with new ideas.
- Play with different drum loops or pre-recorded loops.
- Write down a chord progression from a different style of music and see how it works in the style you're familiar with.
- Notice the contrast of different styles. Is it rhythmic, smooth, or spacious? Apply these concepts.
- Make flash cards of styles. Put them in a hat and pick until something works. Who knows? It might work.
- Try a melodic or rhythmic approach from different styles.
- Get a lesson or two from a local musician specializing in a specific style of music.

- Listen to some music and try to write a song just like it with your own style.
- Notice different techniques, like flamenco, that add different sonic flavors.
- Put two styles together and see what you hear.
- What other ways can you come up with?

____

____

____

____

Let's try some examples and see what comes out. I'll play a part to a backing track, then the next track will have the same part with no bass for your creative endeavors.

Pop/Latin – pop song with a Latin feel

Metal/Funk - Metal song with a funky bass line

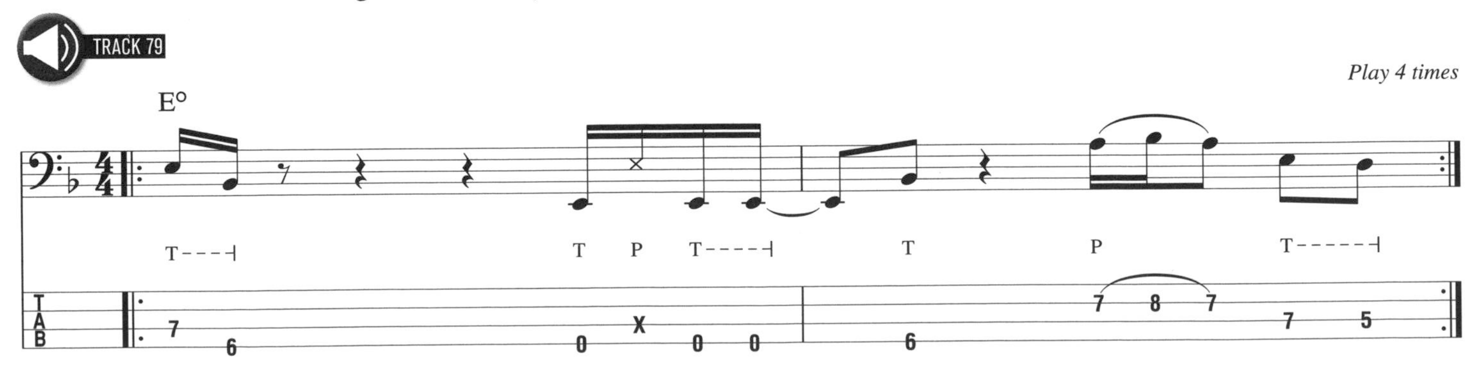

Rock/Blues – Rock song with a blues progression

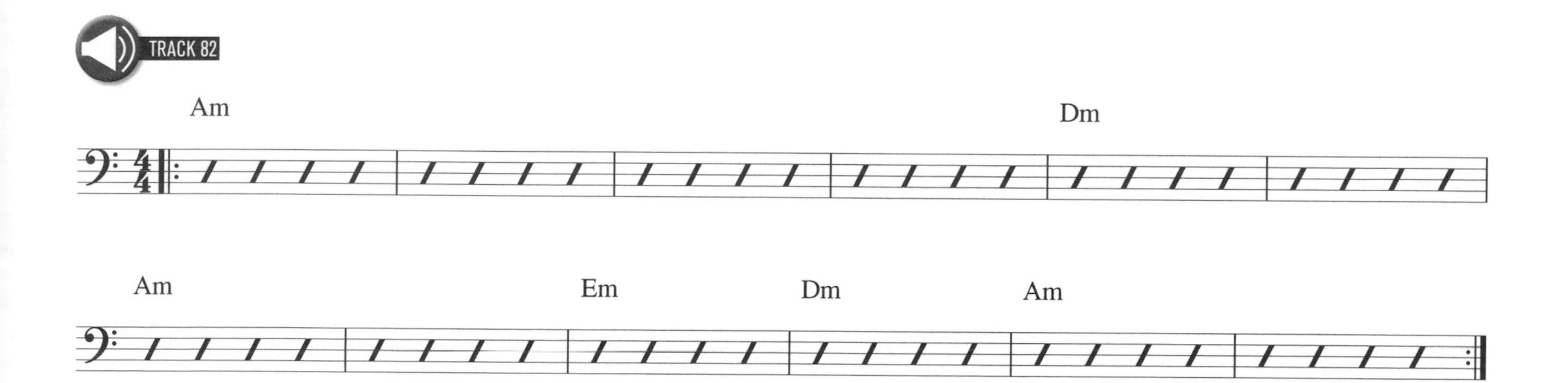

Fusion Rock/Eastern – Fusion rock groove with an Eastern scale

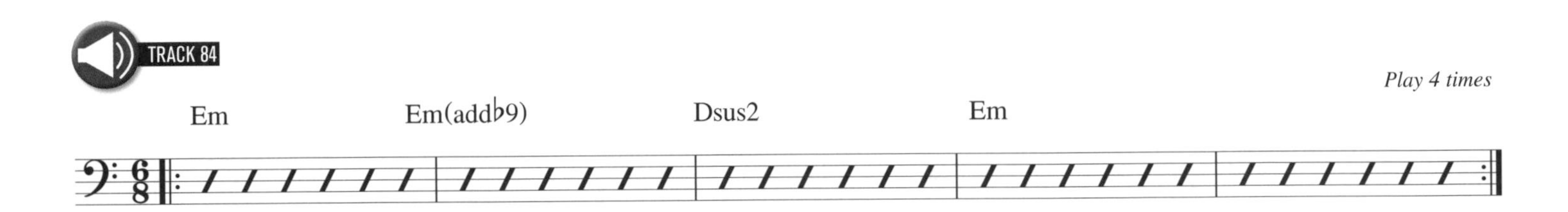

These just scratch the surface of possible ideas. When using different styles, just be open to trying things. If it doesn't work, move on. If it does, explore and have fun with it.

Listening

Listening is the most important concept of the book. It's the simplest to explain, yet the hardest to apply. Listen. Use your ears to hear what sounds good to you. Most importantly, listen to the inner you (the little voice inside that is your intuition). Others will always have ideas of what is best, so trust yourself. Will music ever evolve if the ones who pushed the limit listened to others before themselves? No. It's great to get pointers and tips when you are learning. A good motto is when you ask for opinions, take them in, because those are the times you are open and trust the person you are asking. When others offer them unsolicited, especially if they try to bring you down, thank them and then let it go. Twenty people will have twenty different opinions and, if you are trying to please twenty people, you'll be chasing around approval for the rest of your creative life. At that point, you lose your creative voice.

Humming & Singing

Another form of tapping into creativity, even if you aren't a good singer, is singing or humming an idea before you play or while you play. Singing connects the internal to the external; it helps to translate what you hear on the inside. If you find the groove lacking, a solo not working, a bass line not fitting, or if you feel disconnected from the music, it is a great way to plug back in. Try it out on the next example. Listen to the example before you touch your bass, hum or sing an idea, then play what you sang.

Don't skip this! Give it a try and see what happens.

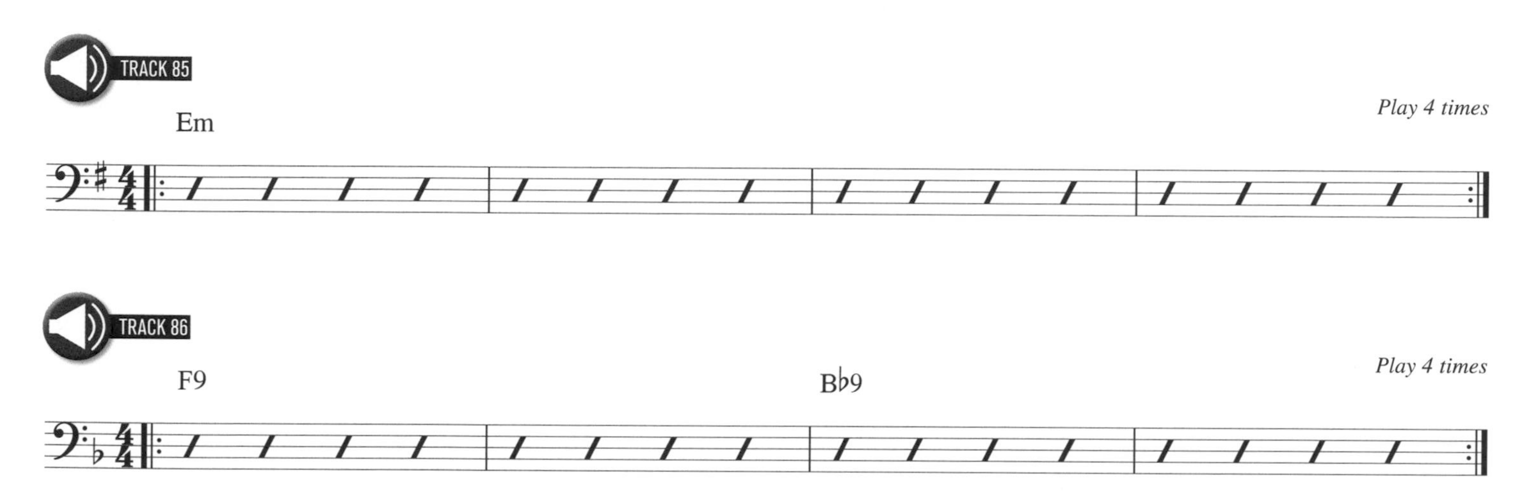

The purpose of the examples in this book is to spark ideas. If they aren't your style of music, write your own and try even harder to come up with ideas. There are millions of tools to create with out there (computers, sequencers, recorders, drum machines). You name it, they probably have it. Become familiar with some of these tools because they are invaluable.

Following the Melody

Another way to create bass parts that continue to evolve is by learning the melodies to the songs you are playing. If you know the melody, you can hint at it rhythmically or melodically in a fill or groove. Jazz musicians do it all the time. By really knowing the songs, they can play around the melody, which makes the song more exciting for the band and the listener.

Here are some ways you can follow the melody:

- *Call and response.* The melody is performed as a figure and you respond with a similar melody in a fill.
- *Catch rhythm.* The melody is performed as a specific rhythm and you play the same rhythm at the same time using a root note or different notes.
- *Write a part.* Create a line or phrase that implies the melody.
- *Imply different melodies in solos.* We've all heard it before when a soloist implies a melody from a different song within a solo.
- *Make a bass melody.* If an original song had a melody that didn't work out but was still good, bring it back as a bass part for a new song; adapt it to bass and make a figure out of it.

- Other ideas?

____

____

____

____

As they always say "melody is king," so the more melodies you know, the easier it will be to create melodic ideas.

Math

Sometimes a mathematical approach can spark new creativity. What I mean by math is to map out riffs from a time signature standpoint, or take lines and use your mind to add or subtract notes and intervals. You can use technical riffs, scales, or warm-ups and make music out of them. There are millions of bands that come up with mathematical ideas that become songs. Some fusion and progressive metal bands have made an art of this approach.

We all use it regardless of being aware of math and music. "Let's play this riff four times then go here for two," or, "this is in 4/4 time then switches to 3/4," and so on. Drummers do it all the time; they play out a rhythm superimposed over another. Keeping time is math. Math and music are linked.

Here are some ways you can use math to develop ideas:

- *Time signatures.* Add a beat or drop a beat to change time signatures. Imply different time signatures over the one you are playing in (e.g., four bars of 3/4 time equal three bars of 4/4 time). Endless possibilities!
- *Drum patterns.* Use different drum rudiments and apply the math to bass techniques.
- *Riffs.* Move notes around, add or drop notes, and come up with riffs based on different note combinations.
- *Writing.* Write parts without listening and see if they work out.
- Other ideas?

____

____

____

____

There are endless possibilities in music and creativity.

Other Instruments

Another creative avenue is to approach bass from a different perspective. Listen to other instruments and apply their approach to the bass. Horn players, woodwind, strings, piano, guitar, sitar, and drums are great resources. If you are a musician, other instruments and musicians inspire you. What is their approach? Take a few lessons, buy some books, transcribe some music and learn what and how they do what they do.

Asking for Help

In music, as in life, most tend to hide what they don't know versus just asking for help. Learning from a teacher can make it a lot easier and will expand your horizons further than I can in this book. Take the time to ask for help if you are frustrated or don't understand something. This is a much better option than giving up. Where there is a will, there is a way.

Finding the Best

In every situation you can learn. Even if the gig was bad you can take it home and work on it. Take the challenge and turn it into a lesson to be learned for the next time. Soon, what once was hard or a problem, no longer is. With that positive attitude, you'll find more people wanting to work with you, and it will be easier to get gigs and create.

Final Words

This book is all about creativity. Not an easy topic to cover. What makes someone creative? I believe everyone is creative equally. We all have creativity. Just like thinking; we all do it. Some are just more open to exploring and doing it; some have blocks and some never really try. I can't stress enough about being open and having a positive approach when creating. If you feel open and positive about it, you will be. If you feel frustrated, you are. In the end it's all up to you.

Blessings,
Chris Kringel
www.kringelbass.com

Bass Notation Legend

Bass music can be notated two different ways: on a *musical staff*, and in *tablature*.

THE MUSICAL STAFF shows pitches and rhythms and is divided by bar lines into measures. Pitches are named after the first seven letters of the alphabet.

TABLATURE graphically represents the bass fingerboard. Each horizontal line represents a string, and each number represents a fret.

Notes:

Strings:
high G D A low E

3rd string, open

2nd string, 2nd fret

1st & 2nd strings open, played together

HAMMER-ON: Strike the first (lower) note with one finger, then sound the higher note (on the same string) with another finger by fretting it without picking.

PULL-OFF: Place both fingers on the notes to be sounded. Strike the first note and without picking, pull the finger off to sound the second (lower) note.

LEGATO SLIDE: Strike the first note and then slide the same fret-hand finger up or down to the second note. The second note is not struck.

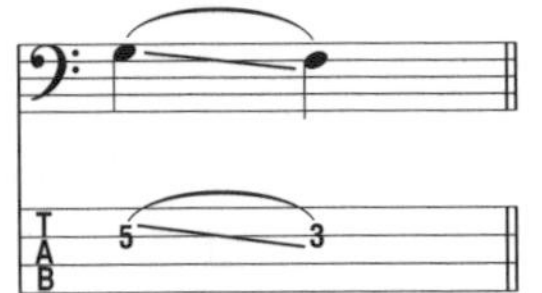

SHIFT SLIDE: Same as legato slide, except the second note is struck.

TRILL: Very rapidly alternate between the notes indicated by continuously hammering on and pulling off.

TREMOLO PICKING: The note is picked as rapidly and continuously as possible.

VIBRATO: The string is vibrated by rapidly bending and releasing the note with the fretting hand.

SHAKE: Using one finger, rapidly alternate between two notes on one string by sliding either a half-step above or below.

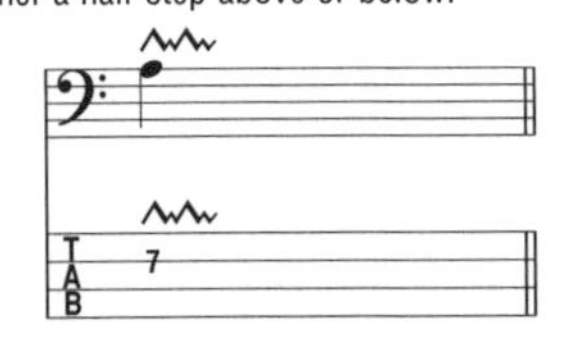

NATURAL HARMONIC: Strike the note while the fret hand lightly touches the string directly over the fret indicated.

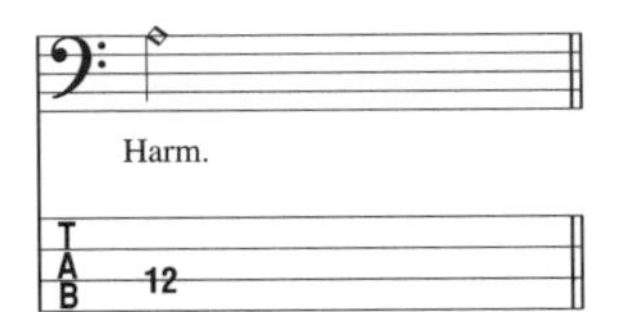

MUFFLED STRINGS: A percussive sound is produced by laying the fret hand across the string(s) without depressing them and striking them with the pick hand.

BEND: Strike the note and bend up the interval shown.

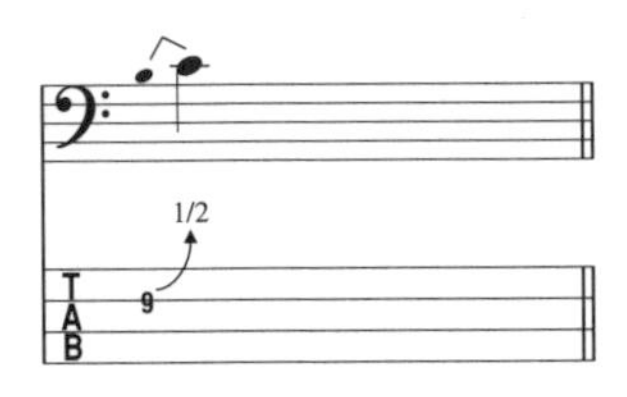

BEND AND RELEASE: Strike the note and bend up as indicated, then release back to the original note. Only the first note is struck.

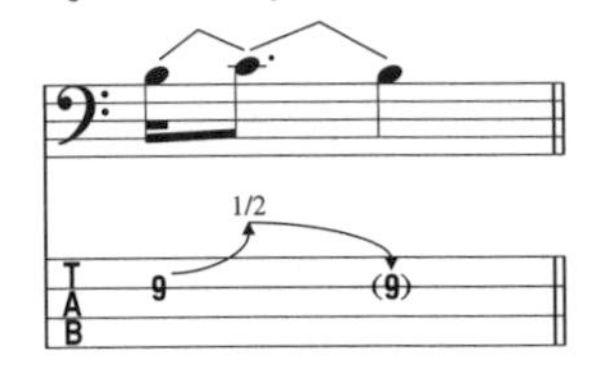

RIGHT-HAND TAP: Hammer ("tap") the fret indicated with the "pick-hand" index or middle finger and pull off to the note fretted by the fret hand.

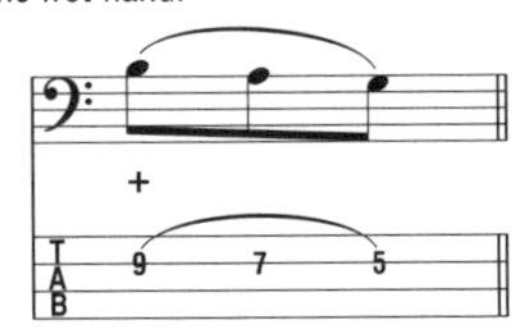

LEFT-HAND TAP: Hammer ("tap") the fret indicated with the "fret-hand" index or middle finger.

SLAP: Strike ("slap") string with right-hand thumb.

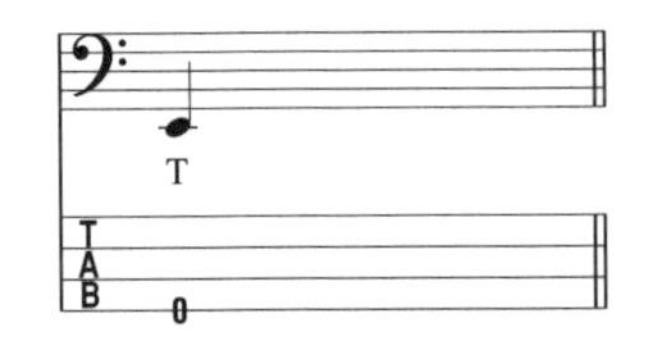

POP: Snap ("pop") string with right-hand index or middle finger.

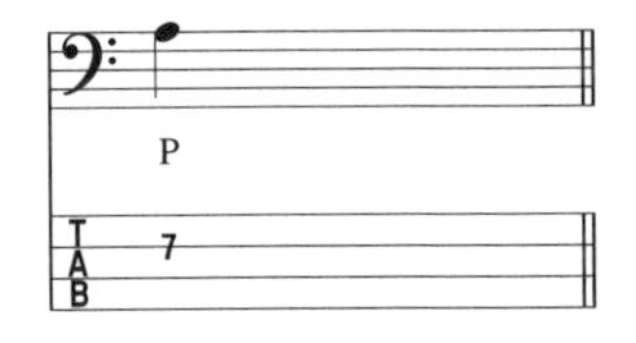

Additional Musical Definitions

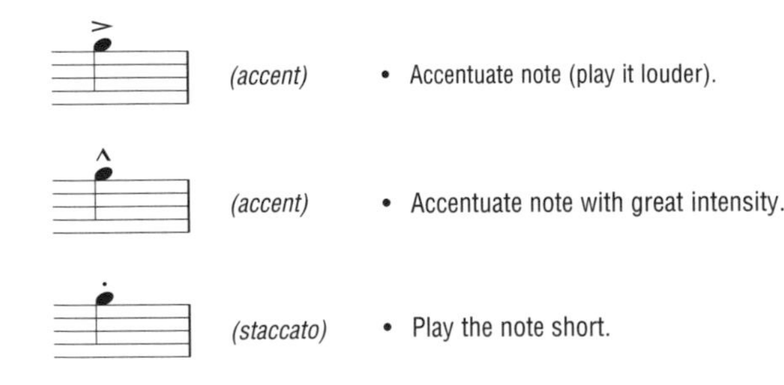

(accent) • Accentuate note (play it louder).

(accent) • Accentuate note with great intensity.

(staccato) • Play the note short.

• Downstroke

• Upstroke

D.S. al Coda • Go back to the sign (𝄋), then play until the measure marked "***To Coda***," then skip to the section labelled "**Coda**."

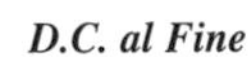

D.C. al Fine • Go back to the beginning of the song and play until the measure marked "***Fine***" (end).

Bass Fig. • Label used to recall a recurring pattern.

Fill • Label used to identify a brief melodic figure which is to be inserted into the arrangement.

tacet • Instrument is silent (drops out).

• Repeat measures between signs.

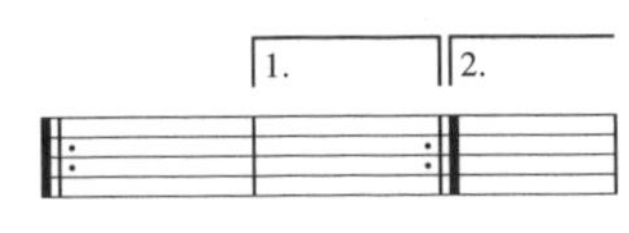

• When a repeated section has different endings, play the first ending only the first time and the second ending only the second time.

NOTE: Tablature numbers in parentheses mean:

1. The note is being sustained over a system (note in standard notation is tied), or
2. The note is sustained, but a new articulation (such as a hammer-on, pull-off, slide or vibrato) begins, or
3. The note is a barely audible "ghost" note (note in standard notation is also in parentheses).

HAL•LEONARD
BASS PLAY-ALONG™

The Bass Play-Along Series will help you play your favorite songs quickly and easily! Just follow the tab, listen to the CD to hear how the bass should sound, and then play along using the separate backing tracks. The melody and lyrics are also included in the book in case you want to sing, or to simply help you follow along. The CD is enhanced so you can use your computer to adjust the recording to any tempo without changing pitch!

1. Rock
Songs: Another One Bites the Dust • Badge • Brown Eyed Girl • Come Together • The Joker • Low Rider • Money • Sweet Emotion.
00699674 Book/CD Pack.............. $12.95

2. R&B
Songs: Get Ready • I Can't Help Myself (Sugar Pie, Honey Bunch) • I Got You (I Feel Good) • I Heard It Through the Grapevine • I Want You Back • In the Midnight Hour • My Girl • You Can't Hurry Love.
00699675 Book/CD Pack.............. $12.95

3. Pop/Rock
Songs: Crazy Little Thing Called Love • Crocodile Rock • Maneater • My Life • No Reply at All • Peg • Message in a Bottle • Suffragette City.
00699677 Book/CD Pack.............. $12.95

4. '90s Rock
Songs: All I Wanna Do • Fly Away • Give It Away • Hard to Handle • Jeremy • Know Your Enemy • Spiderwebs • You Oughta Know.
00699679 Book/CD Pack.............. $12.95

5. Funk
Songs: Brick House • Cissy Strut • Get Off • Get Up (I Feel Like Being) a Sex Machine • Higher Ground • Le Freak • Pick up the Pieces • Super Freak.
00699680 Book/CD Pack.............. $12.95

6. Classic Rock
Songs: Free Ride • Funk #49 • Gimme Three Steps • Green-Eyed Lady • Radar Love • Werewolves of London • White Room • Won't Get Fooled Again.
00699678 Book/CD Pack.............. $12.95

7. Hard Rock
Songs: Crazy Train • Detroit Rock City • Iron Man • Livin' on a Prayer • Living After Midnight • Peace Sells • Smoke on the Water • The Trooper.
00699676 Book/CD Pack.............. $14.95

8. Punk Rock
Songs: Brain Stew • Buddy Holly • Dirty Little Secret • Fat Lip • Flavor of the Weak • Gotta Get Away • Lifestyles of the Rich and Famous • Man Overboard.
00699813 Book/CD Pack.............. $12.95

9. Blues
Songs: All Your Love (I Miss Loving) • Born Under a Bad Sign • I'm Tore Down • I'm Your Hoochie Coochie Man • Killing Floor • Pride and Joy • Sweet Home Chicago • The Thrill Is Gone.
00699817 Book/CD Pack.............. $12.95

10. Jimi Hendrix Smash Hits
Songs: All Along the Watchtower • Can You See Me? • Crosstown Traffic • Fire • Foxey Lady • Hey Joe • Manic Depression • Purple Haze • Red House • Remember • Stone Free • The Wind Cries Mary.
00699815 Book/CD Pack.............. $16.95

11. Country
Songs: Achy Breaky Heart (Don't Tell My Heart) • All My Ex's Live in Texas • Boot Scootin' Boogie • Chattahoochee • Guitars, Cadillacs • I Like It, I Love It • Should've Been a Cowboy • T-R-O-U-B-L-E.
00699818 Book/CD Pack.............. $12.95

13. Lennon & McCartney
Songs: All My Loving • Back in the U.S.S.R. • Day Tripper • Eight Days a Week • Get Back • I Saw Her Standing There • Nowhere Man • Paperback Writer.
00699816 .... $14.99

21. Rock Band – Modern Rock
Songs: Are You Gonna Be My Girl • Black Hole Sun • Creep • Dani California • In Bloom • Learn to Fly • Say It Ain't So • When You Were Young.
00700705 Book/CD Pack.............. $14.95

22. Rock Band – Classic Rock
Songs: Ballroom Blitz • Detroit Rock City • Don't Fear the Reaper • Gimme Shelter • Highway Star • Mississippi Queen • Suffragette City • Train Kept A-Rollin'.
00700706 Book/CD Pack.............. $14.95

23. Pink Floyd – Dark Side of The Moon
Songs: Any Colour You Like • Brain Damage • Breathe • Eclipse • Money • Time • Us and Them.
00700847 Book/CD Pack.............. $14.99

FOR MORE INFORMATION,
SEE YOUR LOCAL MUSIC DEALER,
OR WRITE TO:

HAL•LEONARD®
CORPORATION
7777 W. BLUEMOUND RD. P.O. BOX 13819
MILWAUKEE, WISCONSIN 53213

Visit Hal Leonard Online at **www.halleonard.com**

Prices, contents, and availability subject to change without notice.

0409

Bass Recorded Versions® feature authentic transcriptions written in standard notation and tablature for bass guitar. This series features complete bass lines from the classics to contemporary superstars.

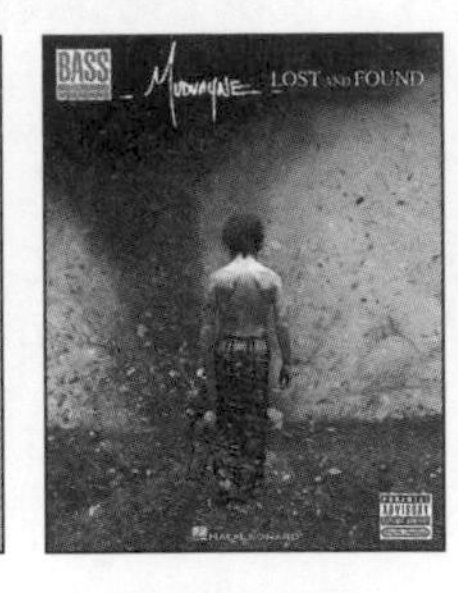

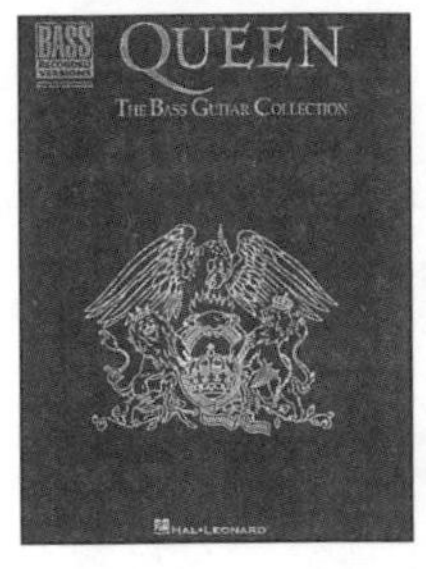

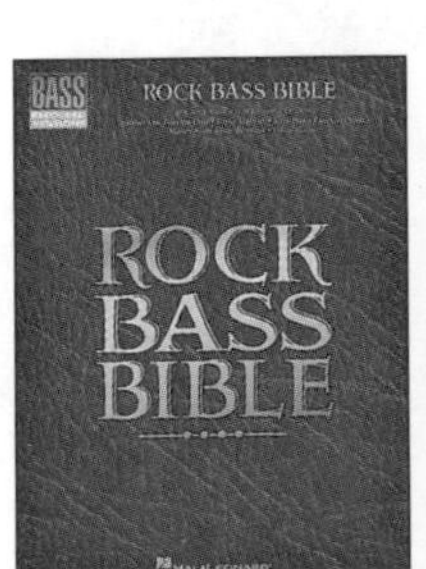

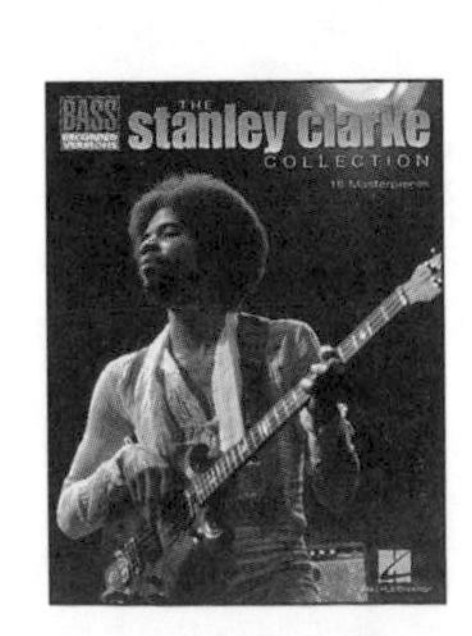

25 All-Time Rock Bass Classics
00690445 / $14.95

25 Essential Rock Bass Classics
00690210 / $15.95

Aerosmith Bass Collection
00690413 / $17.95

Best of Victor Bailey
00690718 / $19.95

Bass Tab 1990-1999
00690400 / $16.95

Bass Tab 1999-2000
00690404 / $14.95

Bass Tab White Pages
00690508 / $29.95

The Beatles Bass Lines
00690170 / $14.95

The Beatles 1962-1966
00690556 / $18.99

The Beatles 1967-1970
00690557 / $18.99

Best Bass Rock Hits
00694803 / $12.95

Black Sabbath – We Sold Our Soul For Rock 'N' Roll
00660116 / $17.95

The Best of Blink 182
00690549 / $18.95

Blues Bass Classics
00690291 / $14.95

Boston Bass Collection
00690935 / $19.95

Chart Hits for Bass
00690729 / $14.95

The Best of Eric Clapton
00660187 / $19.95

Stanley Clarke Collection
00672307 / $19.95

Funk Bass Bible
00690744 / $19.95

Hard Rock Bass Bible
00690746 / $17.95

Jimi Hendrix – Are You Experienced?
00690371 / $17.95

The Buddy Holly Bass Book
00660132 / $12.95

Incubus – Morning View
00690639 / $17.95

Iron Maiden Bass Anthology
00690867 / $22.99

Best of Kiss for Bass
00690080 / $19.95

Bob Marley Bass Collection
00690568 / $19.95

Best of Marcus Miller
00690811 / $19.99

Motown Bass Classics
00690253 / $14.95

Mudvayne – Lost & Found
00690798 / $19.95

Nirvana Bass Collection
00690066 / $19.95

No Doubt – Tragic Kingdom
00120112 / $22.95

The Offspring – Greatest Hits
00690809 / $17.95

Jaco Pastorius – Greatest Jazz Fusion Bass Player
00690421 / $17.95

The Essential Jaco Pastorius
00690420 / $18.95

Pearl Jam – Ten
00694882 / $14.95

Pink Floyd – Dark Side of the Moon
00660172 / $14.95

The Best of Police
00660207 / $14.95

Pop/Rock Bass Bible
00690747 / $17.95

Queen – The Bass Collection
00690065 / $17.95

R&B Bass Bible
00690745 / $17.95

Rage Against the Machine
00690248 / $16.95

The Best of Red Hot Chili Peppers
00695285 / $24.95

Red Hot Chili Peppers – Blood Sugar Sex Magik
00690064 / $19.95

Red Hot Chili Peppers – By the Way
00690585 / $19.95

Red Hot Chili Peppers – Californication
00690390 / $19.95

Red Hot Chili Peppers – Greatest Hits
00690675 / $18.95

Red Hot Chili Peppers – One Hot Minute
00690091 / $18.95

Red Hot Chili Peppers – Stadium Arcadium
00690853 / $24.95

Red Hot Chili Peppers – Stadium Arcadium: Deluxe Edition
Book/2-CD Pack
00690863 / $39.95

Rock Bass Bible
00690446 / $19.95

Rolling Stones
00690256 / $16.95

System of a Down – Toxicity
00690592 / $19.95

Top Hits for Bass
00690677 / $14.95

Stevie Ray Vaughan – Lightnin' Blues 1983-1987
00694778 / $19.95

FOR MORE INFORMATION, SEE YOUR LOCAL MUSIC DEALER, OR WRITE TO:

7777 W. BLUEMOUND RD. P.O. BOX 13819 MILWAUKEE, WI 53213

Visit Hal Leonard Online at
www.halleonard.com

Prices, contents & availability subject to change without notice.
Some products may not be available outside the U.S.A.

0309